In Praise of Inadequate Gifts

A Memoir in Essays

Tarn Wilson

Wandering Aengus Press
Eastsound, WA

First Edition published by Wandering Aengus Press
Nonfiction
ISBN: 978-0-578-86895-0
Library of Congress Cataloguing-in-Publication Data available.
Printed in the United States of America
Cover Image: Biblilogy (detail) by Laura Deem
https://www.lauradeemstudio.com
Author Photo: Anthony Thorton

Wandering Aengus Press
PO Box 334 Eastsound, WA 98245
wanderingaenguspress.com

Wandering Aengus Press is dedicated to publishing works to enrich lives and make the world a better place.

For Benjamin

IN PRAISE OF INADEQUATE GIFTS

A Memoir in Essays

TABLE OF CONTENTS

I.

THE HISTORY OF MY TEETH

1

Hypodontia – a congenital condition marked by fewer than the usual number of teeth.

When I was five, I asked my father if all people have the same number of teeth. He told me that, generally, adults have thirty-two and children twenty, but I was missing some—my upper lateral incisors between my front and eye teeth—probably because my mouth was too small. Irrefutable evidence that I was—as I had suspected—a mutant freak.

In fifth grade, I visited a natural history museum and saw an exhibit on evolution. It began with an oversized drop of primeval ooze, progressed from legged-land-fish through modern humans, and ended with a life-sized model of the predicted human-of-the-future, a creature remarkably similar to the aliens from *Close Encounters of Third Kind*. Tall. Sunken chest. Skinny arms. Long fingers. Large eyes. And, because we no longer needed big teeth for ripping raw flesh, a small mouth.

I was tall and skinny. I had long fingers and big eyes. My mouth was so small, all my teeth didn't fit. I was the shape-of-things-to-come. I was just more evolved than the average child.

Five percent of the time, I believed my evolution argument; for the other ninety-five, I was sure I was deformed.

2

Midline Diastema – a gap between the two front teeth.

My front teeth, which already looked too long and large next to my eyeteeth, also had a gap between them.

The space had its benefits: When my sister and I were in elementary school and took baths together, I'd squirt water between my teeth into her face, and she'd scream, "You're spitting on me!"

In Praise of Inadequate Gifts

And I'd squirt her again, which would start another water-splashing, shaving cream fight. It also amused her when I carried small sticks in the gap.

But mostly, the space between my front teeth made me feel ugly. I hated my school pictures. Every year I hoped that *this* time I'd be beautiful. But always, that pale, thin face; that hair too short and choppy; and those two rabbity teeth.

3

Malocclusion – misalignment of the teeth, which can be caused by thumb sucking.

When did my teeth obsession begin? Before I began school, I rarely thought about teeth. At that time, my hippie parents were attempting an experiment in living off the land on a rural Canadian Island and paid no attention to appearances. My sister and I wore dirty clothes, if we wore them at all, and rarely brushed our hair—or teeth.

Once a month, though, when we drove to town to pick up supplies, the town folks, mostly mining and logging families, would watch me suck my thumb and shake their heads. "If she doesn't stop, her teeth are going to grow in crooked. Have you tried Tabasco sauce?"

I knew that my parents—who told me only half-joking, "You can't trust anyone over thirty"—wouldn't take child-rearing advice from anyone who ate white bread. So I didn't believe the town people.

4

Exfoliation – the process of shedding the deciduous, or baby teeth.

Maybe my obsession began with the physical sensations of those first loose teeth. At first, the tooth would move, just a little. I pressed it with my tongue and rocked it with my finger until I pushed up the first sharp edge. I ran my tongue over and over the sharpness, the opening to a cave. When it loosened, I sucked it up then popped it back into place, like a puzzle piece.

Finally, I twisted it until it hung by just one root. I didn't have the courage for the last pull, but neither could I leave it alone. So I massaged the tooth with my tongue until my gums were numb and the tooth hung by a thread. At last, one gentle tug and the release. Then the raw hole: tender, too soft, tasting like metal with a slight electric charge.

But that can't fully explain my fixation, as almost all children are entranced with their loose teeth—and the strangeness of losing what had seemed as permanent as bone.

5

Disclosing tablets – red dye used to reveal invisible dental plaque.

Or perhaps my obsession began with the arrival of the Teeth People— a young man and woman paid by the province to visit rural classrooms and teach children about proper oral hygiene.

The Teeth People brought an oversized model of white, even teeth set in pink plastic gums. With an oversized toothbrush, they showed us how to brush: hold the bristles at a forty-five degree angle at the gum and stroke to the end of each tooth, at least five times. We should brush our tongues, too, to keep our breath fresh. They showed us how to properly wrap dental floss around our fingers and scrape between our teeth.

As they left, they gave us each a gift packet—a child-sized toothbrush, a miniature container of dental floss, and a packet of plaque-exposing pills. The Teeth People urged us to brush our teeth twice a day and teach our families what we'd learned.

At home, I couldn't get my father to stop working. He mumbled something about the bourgeoisie and schools telling him how to raise his children. My mother listened and nodded, not because she was interested, but because I cared so much.

I stared at my family's mouths. My father had wide, strong teeth, a little crooked, mostly hidden by a straggly blonde mustache. My mother had perfect teeth: straight, white, no spaces, in perfect proportion. My sister—two years younger—had small, bright, far apart teeth, like little pearls.

My sister was only interested in the red pills, which came two-by-two in foil wrappers. I explained we'd brush our teeth as best as we could and the red pills would tell us where we'd missed.

I brushed my teeth twice, paying attention to each tooth. I brushed my tongue, all the way to the back. Proper oral hygiene was hard work. I showed my sister how to floss. I wrapped the string around her finger, but it kept unwinding. I wrapped my own string too tightly and my fingertip turned bright red, then deep red, then purple.

"If I don't take it off," I said to my sister in my best teacher voice, "my finger will die and fall off."

We dissolved the pills in our mouths. I was certain I'd come out clean and white.

"That can't be very good for you," my mother said, followed by a mini-lecture on the dangers of red dye number two.

My sister and I examined each other's mouth. "Your teeth are red," my sister said.

"No they're not." I grabbed my mother's hand mirror. Sure enough, although paler than my sister's, each of my teeth was a sticky red at the gum line. I stretched out my tongue. It was lollipop-red with a broken crack down the center. I brushed my teeth again and again, but the dye persisted for days.

I brushed and flossed every day until my dental floss ran out.

"It doesn't matter," my father said. "They're mostly baby teeth. They'll all fall out."

I thought I was clean and whole, while all this time invisible decay had been eating my teeth.

A month later, my mother left my father. I hadn't seen it coming.

6

Power-biters – children who bite others because they have a strong need for autonomy, power, and control.

Not long after, my sister and I followed my mother to Vancouver where we lived for a time with my mother's friend Nancy and her daughter Geneva.

Geneva, who was also in first grade, was everything I was not.

Even though she was smaller and two months younger, she was loud and bossy. I loved to look at her: olive-colored skin, almond shaped eyes, and a tall, soft afro.

New to the city, I was afraid of everything—crowds, sirens, traffic, the complex maze of streets—but Geneva could take the bus by herself to her dance lessons, speak a little Chinese, do a few kung fu moves, paint her fingernails with red polish, and explain to me the more intimate details of various family members' sex lives.

She had gotten in trouble several times in school for biting the other children—and her teacher. When her mother, in her gentle way, tried to talk to her about it, Geneva bit her too.

When Geneva asked me to clean her room, I did.

"You don't have to do everything she tells you," my mother whispered, a little worried about the strength of my character.

But I wasn't afraid of Geneva's bite. I just wanted to be in the presence of this force-of-nature who knew how to use her teeth to get what she wanted.

7

Most Americans didn't regularly brush their teeth until after World War II, when returning soldiers, trained by the military, brought the habit home.

By third grade, my mother had moved us back to Colorado and my sister and I visited my father in the summers. He'd often quit his latest job so we could live in a teepee, a treehouse, an old fishing boat. The summer we camped for a month on the beach, he became angry when I asked to wash my feet before I put them in my sleeping bag. "Your mother has made you soft." He grew angry again when I wanted toothpaste. "You don't need to brush your teeth every night," he said. "That's middle-class shit. Indians brushed their teeth with sticks."

I still wanted to be clean, but then I was ashamed of my want, as if it were some sort of weakness, like being a girl when your father wanted a boy.

8

Before the invention of nylon in the late 1930s, toothbrush bristles were made of boar or horsehair.

When I was in fourth grade, my teacher wanted students' fathers to speak to our class about their careers. My father happened to be in town on a rare visit and had recently started a computer business, which at the time was new and interesting, so I invited him.

He agreed, and I started to worry. He didn't look like the other suburban fathers. His teeth had grayed near the gums. His wavy blond hair was always greasy at the roots. I figured asking him to give up his rumpled jeans was too much, but I did muster the courage to whisper, "Before you visit my class, will you take a shower and brush your teeth?"

He didn't reply.

And he never came.

9

The town people were right.

In fifth grade, I was still sucking my thumb before I fell asleep, and sure enough, my rabbit teeth with the space between them began to twist.

10

In Nigeria, spaces between the front teeth are considered beautiful, and some people have cosmetic dentistry to create them.

When I was in seventh grade, my mother thought I should get braces. I already had acne and I didn't want a mouth full of silver, but neither did I want to become a twisty, gap-toothed adult. And I wanted boys to like me, although I wouldn't confess that to anyone. I also thought that people with funny teeth didn't look as smart as people with straight teeth. And even more than wanting to be beautiful, I wanted to be smart.

My father didn't want to pay. "More middle-class bullshit. What does she need braces for? Her teeth are just fine. They aren't hurting her, are they?"

"You don't understand," my mother tried to explain, "what

In Praise of Inadequate Gifts

it's like to be a girl."

"You aren't going to let her buy into all that shit, are you?"

I didn't want to be frivolous. I didn't want to be expensive. And yet I knew that there are some things that make moving through the world easier. Besides, my father always fell for beautiful women—not crazy-toothed ones—so I had a sneaking suspicion that while my father was making me feel like a woman of insubstantial character, his primary motive was avoiding the cost. So I stood, equally balanced between guilt for my feminine vanity and frustration at my father for all the things he hadn't been willing to give us. Child support. Shoes for the first day of school. A phone call on my birthday. Letters telling us he thought of us.

11

My mother agreed to split the cost.

My orthodontist was a wannabe cowboy. He wore a Stetson hat and plaid shirts and lived on a large ranch.

When I complained my teeth were aching, he answered, screwing my braces a little tighter, "Little lady, if ya wanna find yerself a husband, wer gonna have to fix these teeth."

I was quiet. Still imagining myself a woman of depth, when he took his fingers from my mouth, I answered, "I hope the man I marry doesn't love me for my teeth."

"Honey," he answered in his affected western drawl, "ya gotta catch one first 'fore he can appreciate ya for yer finer qualities."

12

obsess - 1503, "to besiege," from L. obsessus, pp. of obsidere "besiege, occupy," lit. "sit opposite to," from ob "against" + sedere "sit." Of evil spirits, "to haunt," is from 1540. Obsession was originally (1513) "the act of besieging," then "hostile action of the devil or an evil spirit" (1605); meaning "persistent influence or idea" is first recorded 1680. – Online Etymology Dictionary. www.etymonline.com

My sister's teeth grew in perfectly: white and well-proportioned with no spaces between them. She had a wide, movie star smile.

In Praise of Inadequate Gifts

Then, when my sister was in fifth grade, a stranger broke into our house and molested her.

Afterward, while I slept and my sister lay frozen in terror, the stranger raped our mother.

We moved from Denver to Boulder, and my sister and I—trembly and disoriented—changed schools in the middle of the year. Compared to the college-town kids, we were poorly dressed and undereducated. My sister already had hints of a woman's body, so a classmate called her fat.

At night, my sister would brush her teeth for half an hour. Then floss. I'd watch her as she carefully dried each tooth with a washcloth.

13

Me? I bit my forearm, from the wrist toward the elbow. Harder, harder, harder, daring myself—the skin so thin between my teeth. The next day a row of purple half-circles lined my arm. In school, while a teacher droned, I'd raise my sleeve a little to see if the circles were still there. I pressed the tender teeth marks, frightened and fascinated by the person who'd do such a thing.

14

LONDON, Jan 29 (Reuters Life!) - Straightening children's crooked teeth with braces may improve their smile but it is no guarantee of happiness and improved self-esteem. A 20-year study by scientists in Britain that looked at the impact of braces on more than 300 children in Wales showed that having straighter teeth had little positive impact on their psychological health later in life.

Patricia Reaney

At the end of tenth grade, my orthodontist removed my braces and sent me to the periodontist. The Cowboy explained we have ligaments attached to our teeth, which act like natural rubber bands, and we needed to snip mine or they'd pull my front teeth back apart.

This procedure worried me: without ligaments, would my teeth become loose and sloppy? But neither did I want a gap so big I could shoot water through it.

15

The eyeteeth got their name because they fall just below the eye. They are also called upper canines, cupids, dogteeth, and fangs.

My junior year, we moved to Colorado Springs, where I attracted the attention of the boy I wanted, a soccer player who lived across the street from my new house.

I loved his teeth. His mother was Puerto Rican and petite, his father stocky and Polish. He had his father's wide face, too old for a teenager, and a mouth so big he could stuff in a whole McDonald's hamburger. I have a photograph of the two of us on a ski slope. His eyes are chestnut brown and his grin is laugh-out-loud wide. His teeth are straight and even, except for his eyeteeth, which are a little longer and slightly pointed.

Although my passion for him has long since faded, I still want to kiss those eye teeth.

16

"Gap-toothed was she, it is no lie to say."

Canterbury Tales

In junior English, we were reading *Canterbury Tales*, and our teacher explained some medieval lore: the space between the Wife of Bath's teeth signified that she was highly sexed.

What did this mean about me? In my relationship with my new boyfriend, I was constantly monitoring the murky line between yes and no, stretched between my body's longing and my fears about risks to my heart and future. I was a good girl, going places. That was the story I told myself. Did my formerly gapped teeth mean I, too, was highly sexed? Did my now-closed teeth mean that I was highly sexed, but had hidden it from the world? Was I hiding it from myself?

17

Before my junior year ended, my perfect teeth began slowly creeping apart. Even without their ligaments, they had a memory of their own, their own stubborn resistance to change. We had run out of teeth money, so there was nothing to do but leave them to their slow journey home.

My senior year, my boyfriend left for college and my art teacher developed a crush on me, although I wouldn't realize it until later. He was a new teacher: tall, dignified, handsome, often exasperated by teenagers, a perfectionist, our football coach, a Kansas farm boy, and an exquisite colored-pencil artist.

Of course, I must have considered that it wasn't typical for a senior girl to hang out with a young, single teacher, go to his apartment, to the movies.

When I turned in my assigned self-portrait, he said, "Look, you even drew the little gap between the front teeth." By the sweet, careful way he said it, I knew suddenly that he had looked at me closely, the way you do with someone you love, and I felt shame for what I hadn't yet been able to admit to myself: I had attracted the attention of a forbidden man.

18-21

English –	*Wisdom Teeth*
Turkish –	*Twentieth Year Teeth*
Arabic –	*Teeth of the Mind.*
Korean –	*Love Teeth, for the age of first love*
Japanese –	*Unknown to Parents Teeth*

My upper wisdom teeth never formed. My lower wisdom teeth were pulled when I was nineteen. Four absent wisdom teeth. I honor what is missing. Wisdom. Fathers.

22

Those who have studied the reports of alien abductions say that the "gray" aliens, the ones with silver-black skin and large almond shaped eyes, have a small, slit-like mouth, no tongue, and cartilage instead of teeth.

Years later, in the middle of my first marriage, which was often shaky, I sometimes suddenly felt as if I were an alien, seeing the human form for the first time: the bare, freckled skin. Jointed arms and legs.

Stretched drips of fingers and toes with crispy nails on the end. Bulbous heads with long fur. Twisted fungus ears. Two rolling marble eyes. All of these were odd and ugly, but mouths were downright disgusting: fat lips opening to a cavernous hole with a tongue thick and wiggly as some sea creature. Teeth like chips of exposed bone, something that should be hidden in a private space, not right in the middle of one's face.

"Look!" I said to my husband. I was lying on my back on the living room floor, having just finished watching a movie. I bared my gapped teeth, wiggled my tongue and stretched my fingers and toes in his face. "Humans are *so* weird!"

"*You* are weird," he said.

23

Diagnostic Criteria of Body Dysmorphic Disorder (BDD) According to DSM-IV: Preoccupation with an imagined defect in appearance. If a slight physical anomaly is present, the person's concern is markedly excessive.

In my first decade of teaching, several of my high school students with impaired social skills told me—not as an insult but as a cheerful observation—that I looked like a rabbit. Some days, when I caught a glimpse of myself unexpectedly, perhaps in the rearview mirror or a store window, and saw my teeth, I felt so ugly for the rest of the day I could barely concentrate.

Some days, when I woke in the morning, the gap between my front teeth seemed wider than usual. Perhaps I'd been swallowing all night and pressing my tongue-too-big-for-my-small-mouth against the inside of my teeth. On these days, or on the mornings of special occasions, I sometimes tied my front teeth together with dental floss or wrapped them with a rubber band to squeeze them together. It shouldn't have work. But it did. I didn't do it too often—I was afraid I might loosen them and they'd fall out. I was a little disturbed, too: Teeth shouldn't be able to move like that.

Then I noticed that when I closed my mouth, the line between my two top and two bottom teeth didn't match, and were, in fact, a

In Praise of Inadequate Gifts

full quarter inch off. Another secret deformity.

At the same time, I saw a documentary on beauty that proved mathematically that the faces and bodies of beautiful people are governed by certain principles. As a side note, the scientists also noted that the bodies of world-class athletes have an almost perfect degree of symmetry. If I ever wanted evidence of why I can't run faster, I just have to look at my crooked smile.

But worse, this discovery made me realize that *none* of my teeth fit together particularly well, and because of this, I often leave my mouth hanging open just a bit. Whenever I was quiet and alone, particularly driving, I obsessed: How could I face my students when I can't even close my mouth?

So why didn't I pay to get my teeth fixed? I heard the voice inside me—is it my father's?—saying "frivolous, frivolous, frivolous." The voice says, "You are such a girl. You care too much for appearances. Think of the useful things you could do with that money."

24

The name "molars" comes from the Latin "mola," meaning millstone, as most mammals use their molars to grind.

Don't think I didn't know my obsession was a little crazy.

At every moment, someone in the world is being raped, beaten, cheated. Someone is hungry, dying, grieving. Someone has lost a home, a limb, a child, a country, this year's crops. Somewhere, a bomb explodes, a vote isn't counted, a sniper hits his mark. We pour our poisons; tigers, polar bears, and desert tortoises move one season closer to extinction.

In the face of so much suffering, why did my thoughts turn obsessively toward teeth?

Perhaps my teeth were merely tangible objects on which to project my formless fears about the great mass of suffering for which I could envision or offer no solutions. If I somehow got rid of my teeth obsession, my misplaced anxiety would likely attach to something else. Say, my inner thighs.

25

The Word becomes flesh. The fears become teeth.

26

Did salt's teeth come
from a bitter mouth?

Pablo Neruda

Not long before my father died, I looked at his teeth, which I hadn't really noticed for years. "Hey," I said, "Your top and bottom teeth don't match up, just like mine." His drinking and smoking had turned them yellow and gray.

My father, who made fun of me for wanting to brush my teeth, for any concession to beauty, answered, "Don't look . . . they embarrass me."

27

Historians have conjectured about Mona Lisa's teeth. She may have ground her teeth at night, worn them down to stubs. Or they're stained black from the mercury cure for syphilis. One dentist says she has the smile of someone who has lost her two front teeth.

My obsession spilled onto other people. I worried about the Mona Lisa's teeth. I stared into the mouths of strangers.

When I was asked to teach a writing retreat for women, I first noticed how many participants had odd teeth. Inched together and overlapping. One row shorter than its opposite row. Even as I noticed these oddities, I was horrified with my shallowness. Even more, I was certain—and I was right—that by the end of the retreat, when I had come to know the women, they would no longer be their strange teeth. I almost couldn't wait for the retreat to be over so I could see these women as more than their mouths. Sure enough, by the end of our time together, talking, listening, writing and sharing stories, their every molecule had become beautiful.

28

I have heard that in France, gapped teeth—called "les dents du bonheur," the teeth of happiness—are considered lucky.

I tried to improve my dental-esteem. I kept a mental list of beautiful people with gaps between their teeth: Lauren Hutton, Amelia Earhart, Madonna. On the web, I found but did not join, groups celebrating gap-toothed beauty.

29

Not long before we divorced, my ex-husband and I went for a hike in the Santa Cruz Mountains and found a deer skull with two remaining teeth. I tugged at the first tooth and it fell into my hand. Long smooth roots and cracked enamel. Shaped like a broken and worn seashell. I pulled the smaller, second one and it too released. A dark cavity in the center. Intimate evidence of another creature's life and death.

I wanted to take the teeth home, scrub them with soap and a brush and display them on a shelf above my writing desk.

My husband, who believes in leaving nature intact, wanted me to leave them behind.

I held them in my palm. Little sad jewels, clicking together.

"But I'm writing an essay about teeth."

"Do what you like." He looked away. "But at least ask the deer if he needs them."

I looked at the skull. I tried to wiggle them back into place, but I couldn't find the right angle. I left the teeth behind, loose and crooked in their dried sockets.

30-31

I was born without my upper two lateral incisors. I honor the gaps. I honor what remains absent or delayed. Answers. Beauty. Control.

32

And at whom does rice smile
with infinitely many white teeth?

Pablo Neruda

Here, I break the unwritten rules of essay writing. I'm not supposed to show you the movie camera at the edge of the scene. But I have no other way to tell you the whole story. For a year, this essay didn't have an ending. A puzzle I couldn't solve. Deer molars I couldn't shove back in place.

But after confessing all my teeth stories and tucking the pages away, a miracle happened. My obsession shed as naturally as baby teeth. I no longer tied my front teeth together, or stared at my students' mouths, or feared, when I caught an unexpected glimpse of my face, that I wouldn't be able to make it through the day in such gap-toothed ugliness.

A year later, when my dentist requested I get a bottom retainer for the health of my teeth, I added a top one and closed the space between my front teeth. Obsession imprisons us in repetitive thinking; after my obsession eased its grip I was able to take action.

Maybe writing about my obsession was the equivalent of pressing my tongue over and over against my loose tooth—against what felt strange and uncomfortable and shameful. The soft skin underneath toughened, and when I finally felt brave enough, I twisted, gave a gentle tug, and my obsession released.

Maybe the writing was a disclosing dye, revealing some of what has been invisible to me. Perhaps I let go when I finally understood: when I saw my red teeth next to my parents' separation, the rape next to my sister drying her teeth with a washcloth, how anxiety can find peculiar places to stick.

But these are guesses. Thirty-two sections in honor of thirty-two human teeth. And those that are missing. Arrange them next to each other. Still, I have gaps. Mysteries. Wisdom I'll never have.

This I can say: I'm neither a mutant freak, nor highly evolved. My mouth has morphed into the smile of an ordinary person.

MY PERFECT LITTLE LIFE

The summer I was twenty, I worked in a factory soldering circuit boards for Chrysler LeBarons. I hadn't a clue how a circuit board functioned. Electricity was, and still is, a mystery to me. *Resistors. Transistors. Capacitors.* Words from a language I'd never understand.

This is what you should know: I loved the work. I went to the supply room for my stack of green circuit boards—punched with holes, crossed in copper tracks—and my tray full of components: Black rectangles with curved legs like centipedes. Pretty, striped glass beads with wires on the ends, stamped with little numbers. I loved them like, as a child, I'd loved my mother's jar of brightly colored buttons.

I followed the instructions, matched number to number, and wiggle-snapped the components into place. From the top, the board looked like a city, like flying on an airplane and looking down at the crisscross and curves of streets, the rectangular roof tops, oval tracks, and green baseball fields. I was a god, looking down on a perfect little world.

I'd gotten the job through a temp agency. I wanted to try something new, something that scared me a little, something physical. So instead of checking *administrative* on my application, I checked *light industrial.* I almost marked both, just to make sure I'd be employed, then stopped. One look at me—female, neat handwriting, looking no older than sixteen—and I'd be imprisoned in a cubicle for the rest of the summer.

The factory wasn't in Boulder, where I was staying with my mother, that charming, Colorado mountain town spilling with artists, college students, outdoor enthusiasts, and ex-hippies. Instead, I drove twenty miles east—through dead grass, tumbleweeds, dust, and the faint scent of sage—to Frederick, a dying mining town on the edge of the Great Plains, that stretch of flat land extending all the way to the Mississippi.

After I placed the components, I flipped the board to the underside where the ends of the components, the leads, poked through the copper circles like a strange, metal forest. I held the iron in my right hand, like a pen, and the soldering wire in my left. I pressed the iron and wire together on the copper circle, called the pad. Instantly, the wire dissolved into mesmerizing silver liquid, a growing orb.

It was careful work. Press the iron too long on the pad, and the pad peeled from the board. Press too long against the wire and the molten lead spilled its boundaries and formed a bridge with its neighbor. Don't press long enough, and little holes formed and the components rocked in their sockets.

In my childhood, my sister and I flew to Canada every summer to visit my father, whose work was as inscrutable to me as circuit boards: felling trees, log salvaging, teaching computer science at a community college, computer mapping the ocean floor, building robotic arms for remotely operated submarines. With each visit, he was more distracted and distant. I missed the attentive, imaginative father of my early childhood who disappeared after my parents' divorce and who now often seemed to forget he had children. Perhaps I took the factory job because I wanted to touch his computer-mechanical mind, where he now lived most of the time. If he couldn't come to me, I'd go to him. But I could never understand the boards as electrical flow. They remained the roads and rooftops I saw from the airplane window on my way to see him.

My first day on the job, I showed up wearing shorts and sandals, my hair curled around my shoulders. The floor supervisor shook his head as if the agency had sent him a monkey. "Don't you know you can burn yourself? Tomorrow, pants and closed-toed shoes. And pull your hair back."

From the first training, I loved soldering. So I only half-noticed the group of floor supervisors huddled together, half-heard their whispered *let her go* and. . . *talk to her . . . should we . . . make any difference . . . no you . . . you.* Finally, a manager slowly approached and showed me I was underfilling the joints. I was embarrassed. They

In Praise of Inadequate Gifts

could have shown me earlier—it was an easy fix—but they were as wary as if I'd been an unpredictable stray dog.

But I got it. And then the boards became Legos, Tinker Toys, and building blocks. But for real. My circuit boards would make each car's time blink, mileage flash, and gas tank level blaze.

This is what you should know: I was full of hope.

I'd been raised by a single mother. She was intelligent and resourceful, had started on welfare and carved a career for herself as a paralegal, but her internal demons kept her on the run. I attended twelve schools and lived in twenty-five houses before I left for college. Always, she imagined the next town would be better. Always the demons followed, and we teetered on the edge of poverty and chaos.

But now, age twenty, I was sure I could build a different life for myself. After high school, I was accepted to an idyllic college, a campus that looked like an English Village, poised on the bluffs of the Mississippi. I'd always been a slow, if enthusiastic, cross country runner, but my freshman and sophomore years I'd done the impossible and run a marathon. Spring of my sophomore year, I'd traveled abroad to study literature in the British Isles.

Spring of my junior year, my best friend and I hiked Virginia and West Virginia on the Appalachian Trail. We had no backpacking experience, no mentors, and little cash, but we'd researched, trolled secondhand stores for cheap gear, and mailed ourselves bulk food. At the end of our trip we stopped in a dying, rural Virginia town to do our laundry. As we tossed our clothes into the machines, we chatted with the owner. She stared at our muddy boots drying in the corner. "Boots," she said. "All you need is a pair of boots, and you are walking right out of this place." She shook her head at the possibility dawning on her, at its simplicity.

That's the lesson I wanted to believe. All you needed was a pair of boots and you could walk right into the life you wanted.

My hopefulness irritated my mother. She could be tender and generous—could say just what I needed to hear—but she was also beset

In Praise of Inadequate Gifts

by black depressions. That summer of my factory job, she was in the midst of a quicksand darkness that wanted company and sucked at me. My college, she warned, wasn't the "real world."

"You and your perfect little life," she'd spit, an accusation she'd repeat many times in the years that followed.

A deep and inarticulate part of me feared my mother was right: Most were doomed to sad, small lives and the chances of escape were slim.

I learned that the temp workers, as poorly paid as we were, earned more than the regulars, the ones who'd worked there for years, the ones who'd trained us and fixed our mistakes. Every month, management didn't order enough materials, so the first few weeks were painfully slow. When the supplies did arrive, all permanent employees had mandatory overtime, without overtime pay. We worked ten to twelve-hour days. Mothers couldn't get home to their children or men to their second jobs. One mother, after she paid for childcare, was left with twenty dollars a month. "Why don't you just quit?" I asked, "and stay home with your kids?" She needed the twenty dollars that much. A pair of boots couldn't walk her into a new life.

At the end of that summer, I got my hair cut in a salon in Boulder. While waiting, I took a survey in a women's magazine: *Will your child be born with a birth defect?* I scored the lowest points in categories except one. *Smoking.* No. *Drinking.* No. *Regular exercise.* Yes. *Vegetarian.* Yes. Then: *Have you soldered circuit boards in a factory without proper ventilation or safety equipment?* Yes. The number of points instantly catapulted me into high risk.

This is what you should know: I was lonely. I had no friends in Boulder, and my best friend and I were no longer speaking. After twenty-four hours a day together on the Appalachian Trail, we'd exhausted each other. My mother had left a trail of mangled friendships, so I didn't know healing was possible, that my friend and I would soon reconcile. I felt only a flat grief I tried to ignore. And the women in the factory ignored me. Most of them were in their twenties and thirties, many single mothers. They huddled together at

In Praise of Inadequate Gifts

their tables, speaking fast-Spanish in intimate and bitter tones. One said the word *Barbie*, tossed her head toward me, and hissed.

And I'd just lost my boyfriend. Tim and I had been together for five years, since my junior year of high school when I moved in across the street from him in Colorado Springs. He was a year older, a stocky soccer player. Not the delicate, haunted type I usually liked. He was solid and aimed for ordinary things: children, a luxury American car, a house in the suburbs—wishes that seemed to me, at the time, little prisons. So I'd always thought of him as temporary, but even as we went to different colleges, we'd stayed together. I'd had adventures during the summers, my winter breaks, and he'd begged me to come home. Over and over, we'd broken up and made up. Just that year I'd begun to admit to myself how much I loved him.

I was afraid of the future. The great abyss of my adult life spread ahead of me, just a year away. My college was a fantasy in the middle of the cornfields. No job waited. With the frequency of my mother's moves, I had no real home. A new picture of my future began to grow, one with Tim in it. He was predictability and comfort. He'd been attending CU Boulder, so that summer I'd intentionally returned to him, to the man I thought would become my husband.

At the beginning of that summer, Tim and I were driving home from a date. With no preface other than ordinary small talk, he blurted: "I don't want to marry you." My world swirled. The vision I'd finally begun to solidify of my future melted into a void of emptiness. And it touched my deepest insecurity: I wasn't worthy of love. My father ignored me because I wasn't interesting enough to love. My boyfriend had only pretended to adore me. I was a fool.

So it came as a relief when one of the factory men patted the empty stool beside him. Steve's dry, blonde hair stuck up every which way, and—like most of the men working at the table, all a decade or more older than the women—his face was prematurely wrinkled by outdoor labor and hard partying. He was a non-stop talker, and by the end of the week our meandering conversation ended with a disagreement on the influence of genetics on personality.

"You're stuck, man. It's all in your genes. You got what you got," Steve said.

I argued, fiercely, that we can be bigger than what we've been given.

In the days that followed, I told the men at my table about my hike on the Appalachian Trail and they shared their stories, talking over each other, trying to match each tale with one more outrageous. Wacky road trips. Encounters with bears and mountain lions. Someone at the table asked where I went on my lunch break. I told them I ran at the local high school track and had run marathons. After the men boasted about a few of their athletic feats, Steve added, "Yeah, I ran a marathon." Excited, I asked him some questions. His answers were vague and his finish time close to impossible. The men moved onto other stories: the time someone foiled a robbery; the time someone committed one. Finally, I leaned toward Steve.

"Did you really run a marathon?"

"No," he answered, without a pause or shame.

No one missed a beat. The stories continued. I was as embarrassed as I'd been the first day. I'd missed the unspoken code. In a world where men spent long summer days soldering circuit boards in a windowless room under dim fluorescent lights, a good story was more valuable than truth.

One day, Steve was sitting at a new table and a stool was open across from him. I plopped down with my boards, prepped my iron, and introduced myself to the man next to me. Ed seemed different from the other men. While they were wiry and sun-dried, Ed was pale and slightly plump, with shiny dark hair. Instead of a ragged flannel, he wore pressed polo shirts. When he spoke, the others listened instead of talking over him.

Over the weeks, Ed began to tell me his life stories. He'd been a prisoner of war in Vietnam. He described his hut, and images from movies unfurled in my mind. *Rambo. Apocalypse Now.* I could see the rubbery trees, feel the humidity press against my skin. Feel the fear as the captors approached for interrogation. He described his escape; my

In Praise of Inadequate Gifts

circuit boards disappeared and barbed wire ripped against my skin. He'd eluded his captors for days—but they'd caught him again. He was silent about what happened next.

Unlike the other factory men, who tried to impress me by interrupting each other with more fantastic stories, Ed listened.

He asked about my relationship with Tim. I told him our history. Though I'm sure the weight in my voice revealed more than I'd intended, I put a positive spin on the story:

"It's probably for the best. We didn't have that much in common."

Ed stopped soldering and watched my face. "He doesn't sound like your type. Why'd you go out with him?"

I didn't yet understand all the complex reasons, so I answered as honestly as I knew: "I thought he was cute."

It was true. When my mother moved us to an ordinary suburban community, I made a commitment to pretend to be a teenager for the two years before I graduated. I'd go to football games and out for pizzas. I'd date the cute boy across the street. He'd be a temporary experiment.

Ed looked at me, with those serious, probing eyes.

"That doesn't sound like you." He was implying I was a woman of depth, of character. Mature. I was flattered he understood me so well.

"I was young," I said.

Not long after, Ed told me he worked as a photographer for *National Geographic*. A dream job. My dream life. As we worked, I asked him question after question. Finally, I was curious about why he worked in the factory. He was divorced, he said, and because of his travel spent most of the year away from his two children, so he took summers off to be near them. Their mother would only let him see them a few hours a day, so he took a job to keep himself occupied.

That night, I told my mother about Ed's real job. She'd already heard the prisoner of war story and was suspicious.

"Are you sure?" Why she didn't call him a liar, I don't know.

"That doesn't sound very likely." Maybe the conviction in my voice threw her. Maybe she didn't want to admit to herself that her daughter, the one she depended on to be intuitive and intelligent, could be so gullible. Maybe she was being gentle with me. Her doubt seemed reasonable, and my belief teetered.

But the next day, in Ed's presence, under the fluorescent lights, ten hours with soldering irons pressed against boards, I believed again.

Ed and I had both done reading in metaphysics, psychic phenomena, and the power of the mind. But I believed if such powers were real, we should only use them for unselfish reasons.

Ed had a different view: "I wanted you to sit here," he told me weeks after we'd met. "I willed you to come and sit in the empty seat next to me, and you did."

Maybe I did feel an irresistible pull to that seat. Part of me was flattered he wanted me near him, but mostly I was worried. Worried his will could interrupt my own.

By asking questions around the question and observing closely, Ed figured out I was a virgin. I don't remember if he teased me, if the other men at the table knew. But he learned something intimate about me, and a line had been crossed.

Several days later, we stumbled upon the topic of lost innocence. I don't remember the context, only that Ed believed innocence, once lost, could never be recovered. I began to argue, but Ed didn't rally his usual, intellectual counter attacks. For the first time, he was wordless. He slumped. Shadow images passed across his face and evaporated. He couldn't look at me. He'd disappeared down a dark and silent path I couldn't follow.

I spoke to him with fierce confidence, "Innocence is something we can regain." I believed this. I believed in transformation and regeneration. I believed we could shed the burdens of the past, no matter how heavy. Ed looked at me, with a child's fear. I think he wanted to believe me. Or a tiny, hopeful part of him believed me.

In Praise of Inadequate Gifts

I reached my foot out to his stool, pressed my shoe against his—against that sorrow, like my mother's, that seemed so dark and hopeless and bottomless. Electricity buzzed between us. I left my foot there for the rest of the shift. Felt his weight and warmth press back.

Before we left, Ed suggested we think of each other at nine that night. That felt wrong, taking our work intimacy home, rolling it into evening hours, into the same house where my mother lived. I felt a little sick, but electric-excited, too. So that night, at nine, in my bedroom, I wrapped my thoughts around him. Held his image in my mind. Thought about innocence that couldn't be lost.

The next morning, Ed said nothing about the night. Just chatted his ordinary chat. But more boring than usual.

"I thought of you at nine," I finally said. He didn't answer. "Did you think of me?"

"Nah," he said, soaking some extra solder from his joint with a wick. "I was too busy. Reading that book I told you about. I forgot."

I felt small and stupid. Manipulated. Rejected. My boyfriend's rejection. My father's rejection.

But I also noticed that Ed wasn't looking at me. His conversation was rushed and surfacey. Maybe he *had* thought of me, but wouldn't tell me. I wasn't sure why. Maybe it had to do with power. To admit he'd thought of me was to yield something to me. I also felt safer. I'd been opening up to Ed, but the opening had closed and it wouldn't open again.

A woman in the factory began acting oddly around me. Both lingering too close and intentionally ignoring me, then blurting into my conversation with angry, confusing non-sequiturs. She was an outcast from the gossipy women. Tall. Unnaturally thin and getting thinner. Her tangled brown hair looked as if it might be coming out in clumps. Not all her sentences made sense. But I had liked her: From the beginning, she had treated me with kindness, a childlike sweetness.

Finally, someone explained she was jealous. She'd dated Ed before I'd arrived. All the women had seen my foot on Ed's stool and were rallying around her. I was profoundly embarrassed. People had seen.

In Praise of Inadequate Gifts

And I'd hurt her feelings.

This also became perfectly clear: A *National Geographic* photographer would have other options in women—he would not have chosen what I suddenly realized was a drug-addicted, slowly disappearing circuit board assembler.

This is what you should know: In the last three years, both my mother and father have died and I've separated from the man I've been married to half my life. Like that strange transition between college and adulthood, when I soldered circuit boards for a summer, the future is an open void. *You and your perfect little life.* In some ways my new life is small and perfect. My small and lovely apartment. My job and friends I love. But the future is also wide and frightening and exciting. I feel the same tensions again, the pull toward safety and the stretch toward possibility.

This also remains: I love the work.

I have not soldered since that summer. But the work I do now, this writing, this assembling, is much the same. The pages shaped like circuit boards. My memories piled on top of each other in a tray. I pull them out. Try to wiggle-snap them into place.

I solder connections. Why did I believe Ed? *I was young, I answered. Press too long against the wire and the molten lead spills its boundaries and forms a bridge with its neighbor.* I link him to my absent father, my trapped mother, my lost boyfriend, my irrepressible hopefulness, my fear of the future, and the deep loneliness I couldn't admit to myself. My fear of being made a fool—and the inevitability of it.

When my story is assembled, always imperfectly, always with a few under or overfilled joints, I look down from the top, as from an airplane. For a moment, I hold the summer-I-soldered-keyboards-for-Chrysler-LeBarons as a tiny world in my hand. A story about stories. Stories that delude and distract. Stories that give us courage. How can I know if the story I've told is true? I can't. But I can tell I'm getting close to truth when I've found the right pattern, made the right connections, and feel an electricity I don't understand that pulses through the sentences and makes the story live.

LOVELAND

Through my open window, I smell tin—prelude to a Colorado rain. All day, the slate-colored thunderclouds have been piling above the Rocky Mountains. By afternoon, they began their slow tumble over the plains. By dusk, they have settled, wet and heavy, over our Loveland subdivision. I'm fifteen. I've changed into my nightgown and am reading a book on my bed, lost in someone else's story. A gust of cold air flips my pages, and I rise to close the window. From the second story, I preside over wide, treeless streets lined with cheap tract homes. All with fake shutters. I hate those shutters, glued open and— even if they could close—too small to cover the windows. In the twilight, the neighborhood feels thin and hollow. The first raindrops dot the asphalt, releasing a smell: hot dust, decaying leaves, pepper.

Then I remember: That morning, while my stepfather, Jim, was out, his mother had called. I'd forgotten to tell him. My mother is in the bedroom, watching a made-for-TV movie; Jim is in the family room, watching shoot-outs and car chases. I drift down the stairs. The blue light from the TV flashes on the ceiling. The dialogue seems too loud, urgent, jumbled.

"Jim?"

He's on his way from the couch to the kitchen. He hasn't heard me.

"Jim?" I step out from the shadowed staircase. He has a new beer can in his hand. He looks confused for a moment, as if trying to remember who I am and why I'm in his house.

"Jim, your mom called. This morning."

He squints. He's gained weight and is wearing his glasses, which make his face look square. The face of the man I've grown to love seemed to have sunk behind this new, fleshy layer.

"Your mom called this morning. While you were gone. She wants you to call her back. I forgot to tell—"

"God damn it." He rocks a little. "You and your *bitch* of a mother . . . My mom. Can call. Any time she wants." The air is sour.

My mother thinks Jim's parents call too early on weekend mornings. She thinks they are controlling and over-involved and that Jim is a momma's boy. I have stumbled into the middle of their argument.

"No, Jim . . . I was—"

"Damn it. Don't argue with me!" He raises his arm.

I can't remember the details of his strike. Where I stood. Where he stood. If he grabbed my nightgown. If I had to pull to get away. If he was aiming for my face or my gut. That memory is still buried. But I do know he is clumsy and slow, and before he can hit me again, I wriggle out the front door and into the rain. He stumbles after me, grabbing. I leap down the stairs and sprint down the frontage road, that secret street parallel to the highway, hidden by a wall of poplar trees.

As I settle into a steady run, my thoughts arrange and rearrange themselves, trying to find the story that can explain what has just happened. First, the events organize into a fairy tale: the innocent, virtuous teenage girl is almost beaten by her evil stepfather. She escapes in the nick of time. Look at her run in her flannel nightgown with the little flowers. Look at her bare feet. Look at the rain just dampening her sleeves. She's good, and although she doesn't know it yet, her goodness will be rewarded.

My mother met Jim, the brother of one of her co-workers, at a company picnic. She'd rarely dated in the nine years after her divorce from my hippie-beatnik father, so I didn't know what to expect from their courtship. I was surprised that Jim won my feminist, socialist, and former anti-war activist mother with bouquets of flowers sent to work and three phone calls a day.

My sister and I weren't jealous of Jim: we were relieved. Someone else could attend to our mother's tearful nights, assuage her money fears, rub her back, and be her friend. Suddenly, we were free to be teenagers, to talk on the phone for hours in hushed whispers—without having to report back to our mother the intricacies of our new relationships.

In Praise of Inadequate Gifts

My mother's fantasy man, she told me, was "a Marlborough Man with a Ph.D." My father had the intellect, but Jim fulfilled her cowboy fantasy. He was masculine in a way my father never was: thick, wavy hair; a mustache; a Western drawl; flannel shirts; and perfectly worn cowboy boots. He was a little short for my mother's liking, just several inches taller than her 5'8", but the way he looked in jeans made up for it. When they met, my mother was beautiful with her large blue eyes, soft blonde hair that waved around her shoulders, full lips, and a long, curvy body. When they married, my mother wore a lavender silk business dress and held a bouquet of silver-purple roses while a recording of "You Are So Beautiful to Me" played in the background. She changed her last name to his.

I run under the streetlights. Light dark light dark light dark. My fairy tale version of my story won't solidify—it keeps breaking into the memory of Jim standing on the front stoop, yelling with slurred regret, "Wait . . . Tarn . . . it's raining!" In truth, I know the danger has passed. If I turn around, Jim will awkwardly apologize and I'll go back to my room. But I run anyway. I want him to feel like a monster. All my surprise and fear and hurt have channeled themselves into running and I'm not ready to give up that long, strong, stretch of muscle, the wet air against my face. I like being a quiet, fast animal in the night.

Before my mother and Jim married, my friend Margaret—who in ninth grade already had large breasts—developed a terrible crush on Jim. She took to wearing tight shirts, inviting herself over, and finding excuses to stay in the same room with him. Although Jim largely ignored her embarrassing attempts at small talk, my mother was so annoyed she finally banned Margaret from visiting when Jim was home.

"I love older men," Margaret sighed when I finally dragged her to my room.

I couldn't imagine finding any male older than high school age attractive. They were too hairy and rough-skinned and strong-smelling. But I was curious about Jim. He was a key to a world that

In Praise of Inadequate Gifts

had always been closed to me: popular and athletic high school boys. Through his confessions about his teenage years, I learned their secrets: they were younger and more insecure than I'd ever imagined.

With Jim in the house, I thought I might teach myself to be an athlete. When my sister and I were small and we lived with our parents in the Canadian wilds, they set us free to run in the woods, climb trees, scramble up boulders, and balance on fences. But they never threw us a ball. So when school began, we became those taunted children, picked last for teams. But with Jim's support, I signed up for co-ed soccer. I was hopeless, but so proud of myself for trying. I started running, with more success. I exchanged my shirt with the embroidered Peter Pan collar for a blue sports jersey with a number on the back and three white stripes on the sleeve. Sometimes I'd even settle on the couch next to Jim and try to watch baseball.

On weekends in Boulder before we moved, I ran errands with Jim in his pick-up truck and listened to his oldies radio station. Yes, the songs were sappy, but they were generally cheerful and easy to learn, and, best of all, they inspired Jim to tell stories about his high school buddies, his old girlfriends, and his adventures as the star pitcher at his Arizona high school. His pitching talent got him into college—and then through college. "Yup. I only went to algebra class two times—and earned myself a B." Afterward, he was recruited for the minor leagues but only lasted a year.

Sometimes he'd drive me by streets his company had paved. "The work's more complicated than you'd think." He was an estimator, and he explained how to determine the slope and angle of pavement, especially for curvy mountain roads. I watched his hands on the steering wheel; his fingers were compact, square at the end, a little furry. His wedding ring still seemed shiny-new, not yet a part of his body. I felt a protective, almost parental feeling for him—for this man who had loved high school, who seemed to have slept through the political uprisings of the sixties, whose pleasures were so uncomplicated and so long ago.

My heels sting from their slap-slap on concrete. The newly wet neighborhood has been transformed into an alternate universe with

In Praise of Inadequate Gifts

silver sidewalks, pewter streets, and dry lawns turned pearl-white. My adrenaline-speed eases, and I settle into a pace I think I can hold forever. Then my fairy tale morphs into a story more bitter, one tinted with pride and a shade of revenge. I'd been the girl picked last for teams; Jim had been the semi-pro athlete. But I'd practiced running while he'd practiced drinking, and now I can run for miles while he, with his new double chin, can't stagger farther than the front porch. He deserves his stumbling ugliness.

The year before Jim met my mother, she'd been raped by a stranger. After months of nightmares and ragged tears, she thought she was recovering, that her marriage was a healthy sign. But just months after the wedding, she began to have anxiety attacks. She couldn't concentrate at her job as a manager in an oil company. Now that she was no longer a single parent, she thought she could afford to quit: "Someone can support *me*, for once."

But my mother and Jim had been too hopeful, and Jim's income wasn't enough to cover the payments on the condo in Boulder they'd just bought. They lost the condo and filed for bankruptcy. Then they couldn't find a rental that would take our two large dogs. My mother was willing to give the dogs away, but Jim, his marriage shaky, was not willing to sacrifice Sam, his curly-eared mutt, buddy and ally in a house full of women.

The final, convoluted solution was that we would rent a house in Loveland, an agricultural community thirty miles north. My mother would take temporary secretarial jobs. My sister and I would commute with Jim for our last couple months of school. In the fall, we'd start school in our new town.

Before we moved to Loveland, I thought I might enjoy it. After all, it was Love Land. My aunt and cousins lived there, and they had a large house on the lake, a motorboat, a trampoline, and a dad. My aunt scared me a little—she turned all her family members' embarrassing mistakes into outrageously funny stories—and I dreaded the time when my blunders would make it into her repertoire. But my cousins were kind to us, and with the lake and big house and green grass, Loveland was, in my mind, a land of peace and abundance. By the time we moved, however, my mother was no longer speaking to my aunt, and we settled on the edge of town where cheap developments crawled into high desert.

At first, I didn't have time to worry about the sad barrenness of our neighborhood. Our days were long. We woke up early for our long commute to Boulder. In the evenings, as we returned, we stared at the long shadows of cows and barns and bales. The corn had grown several inches since morning. Every day I was amazed, and every day I'd comment, "I can't believe how fast the corn grows. It's taller than it was this morning!" I'd trace my finger along the window, as if petting the stalks.

"Yup. Pretty amazing," Jim would answer.

"I wonder if I sat there and watched all day if I could see it grow."

"We should try that someday."

When we moved to Loveland, I was prepared for some goodbyes. I was wearying of my old crew of friends from junior high who—bored by the uneventful stories of their suburban lives—played with drugs, drinking, punk haircuts, heavy metal music, and sex with older men and each other. I didn't judge them; they just made me tired. Real life was hard enough without inventing complications. While they wanted a more dramatic version of their lives, I wanted a sweeter one. I felt tainted by the messiness of my childhood and I, too, longed for a different story of my life: I'd be a good girl.

This is what I didn't want to leave: my new Sunday school teachers, an old couple who were round and smart and not afraid of my questions; my brilliant, Buddhist Latin teacher; my work as a counselor at a science camp for elementary school students; my newly-elected position as president of the Key Club; my enormous Norwegian PE teacher who, when he saw my frustration with volleyball, let me run around the lake instead and encouraged me to sign up for my first road race.

Busy saying goodbye to our old lives, neither my sister nor I had prepared ourselves for what would be the long loneliness of summer.

We had no transportation and we were too young for local jobs. We couldn't even find any children to baby-sit. My mother, angry at God for the betrayals of the last several years, refused to drop me at Sunday school. Most days, the temperature soared over a hundred and our house turned into a dry sauna.

"I can't do *nothing* all summer," I complained to my mother.

"Why not?"

I couldn't describe to her the terrible boredom that had already started to descend. All those thin, sunbaked houses. They might turn to dust and blow away. And I had no way to escape from the thickening tension between my mother and Jim. Nothing to distract me. Nothing to contribute anywhere to make me feel as if I were useful or needed.

"*I* would die for some time off." My mother snorted. "You should be grateful."

Once again, my sister and I became each other's only companions. When we were young and isolated in the wilderness, we had only each other. Sometimes, I needed solitude, and when I retreated, I hurt her feelings. Since my anger was more entertaining than neglect, she'd follow me and imitate whatever I was doing.

I'd throw up my hands and yell, "Don't imitate me!"

She'd yell and throw up her hands and yell, "Don't imitate me!"

But when she reached junior high, our roles switched and everything about me annoyed her: my clothes, my voice, the way I parted my hair, my answer to any question.

But that summer, driven by necessity, we'd reached a fragile truce. The only activity within walking distance was a small public pool. We resorted to reading whatever novels we could find and spending a large chunk of each day lying on the concrete beside the pool. At regular intervals, we'd cool ourselves in water so blue-thick with chlorine we could taste the flavor on our lips all summer. Our tongues turned to glue. The dry-hot air sucked all the moisture from our skin. Our blonde hair frizzed and the ends turned green.

Lying on our towels, head to head, we remembered our

In Praise of Inadequate Gifts

elementary school summer days at the public pool in Boulder. Playing mermaid. Doing handstands in the water. The "deaf sister" game: one of us would pretend to be deaf and the other would speak fake sign language until we elicited the curiosity and sympathy of one of the mothers.

"What a good sister you are," the mother would say to the one of us who could hear. And then she'd whisper, "Was she born that way?"

I don't remember most of what Jim and my mother fought about. Their issues, of course, were much deeper than arguments about what time Jim's mother should call. They were both, I guess, profoundly disappointed. And neither knew how to soothe the other's fears. Jim worried that he wasn't smart enough, that he wasn't a good provider; my mother, that she wasn't worthy of love. She'd lost her father when she was seven and no man was big enough to fill that ache.

I no longer remember the words they hurled at each other, just my awareness that this was a new kind of fighting. When Rima and I fought, we thought we hated each other, but now I saw that there were lines we would never cross, cruelties that would cut too deep. Jim and my mother, on the other hand, aimed for weakness and for blood, for the damage from which a relationship can never recover.

"Crazy bitch!" Jim slammed the front door and squealed away in his truck.

"If he just weren't so god-damned dumb," my mother told me, crying on her bed.

I wanted to take a positive action, to make something of this waste of a summer. I signed up for a 10K race, my fourth. I'd run the Bolder Boulder the year before and had been proud to finish smack in the middle of the pack of Kenyans and grandmothers. My lucky number, I thought, was three—the number of our family members before Jim— so when my bib arrived in the mail with the number 333, I was sure I was destined for a strong race.

The start was ten in the morning, and the day was already

scorching. As soon as the gun signaled the start, I felt as if bricks had been laced to my thighs. I lugged those bricks for an hour in long rectangles around the cornfields. At the awards ceremony, I was presented with a special T-shirt for coming in last. Everyone laughed and cheered. I appreciated their spirit, knew that T-shirt would make a funny story—and was wise enough to recognize a lesson about faith in lucky numbers—but, still, the race felt symbolic: in this flat, hot land, even my smallest gestures were doomed.

I run and the sleeves of my damp nightgown stick to my arms, but I'm mesmerized by rhythms. Thump-thump-thumpety-thump of rain on my scalp and forehead. Thwup-thwup of bare feet on concrete. Breath in, breath out. Up curbs, down curbs. For whole blocks, my chest feels empty and I forget all stories and am left only with animal joy. The joy of my muscles expanding and contracting. The joy of rain on my eyelids. The joy of being hidden in shadows. The joy of escape. The joy of being wrongly dressed. The joy of being alone.

As part of his job, Jim was required to be on the emergency road crew; in the event of a snowstorm, he could be called to plow the roads. "It's beautiful," he said. "The snow at night . . . it's quiet." I could visualize what he didn't have the words to say: the snowflakes in his headlights; the slight squeak of the snow under his tires; the way the snow blanketed fences, bushes, and the tops of cars and silenced all the clicks and snores and buzzes of a modern night.

"Maybe I could come with you. Sometime."

"You bet."

And then under my rain-joy, the more painful memories begin to rise. The ones from which I've been running.

After we moved to Loveland, Jim, who usually drank a couple of beers a night, was soon downing six-packs.

"Jim, you're drinking too much," my mother warned.

"Damn it, Janet, you can't tell me what to do!"

My mother, whose mind was agile, talked circles around him,

baiting him. When Jim's thoughts—already too slow for his liking—tangled and stalled, he grabbed her arm.

Memories of their fights arise only in shards. Already, my mind has buried the images so deeply I cannot place myself in those moments: where I stood, how I reacted. Only later, reading an article in a women's magazine, do I learn about the cycle of abuse, that age-old story. The first slap. The first stunned silence. The next day, the apologies, the flowers. More finger-shaped bruises. The first punch. More flowers. The hands choking her throat.

And my mother, so hungry for the words *I love you I need you you're beautiful*, forgives again and again. She believes his words; she believes he can change. But the violence comes harder and faster. My mother spends most of her time at home in an old nightgown, her face colorless and puffy, smoking and crying. "How does he expect me to get a job like this?" She puts her face in her hands and cries some more.

Wet, snaky strands of hair stick to my forehead, my cheeks, my neck. I'm tiring and my pace slows. My point of view tumbles and I'm no longer the center of my stories. Jim is the main character, and he's a fallen hero, a breaking, broken man. It's a story too sad to bear, and I can't hold it for more than a moment.

My sister and I talked about the fights only once, and obscurely. On a Saturday afternoon, in the midst of one of their brawls, my mother lifted a houseplant—a large, happy one with heart-shaped leaves—and hurled it against the wall. The pot shattered and the plant collapsed in a tangled heap on the carpet. The little white roots, poking out from the earth, looked startled to feel light and air.

My mother, still in her nightgown, ran halfway up the stairs, then turned to give Jim a look of pure hatred. Hatred seems too abstract, too overused a word, but I have no other for that glare, which although directed at Jim, bore into my memory. It sucked all the color from her face, her lips, even her hair. Her cheeks had fallen, like an old man's. She held his eyes for a long moment before stomping up the stairs and slamming her door.

In Praise of Inadequate Gifts

Jim, in turn, slammed the front door and screeched away.

My sister and I, suddenly alone, looked at each other. Then looked at the plant. It seemed so disoriented, so alive, so in danger—a goldfish flung from its bowl.

"Wanna replant it?" I asked.

"I was just thinking the same thing!"

We swept up the plant and handfuls of dirt and carried them to the garage, where my mother had stored some empty pots and potting soil. The tidy garage was Jim's domain. A tall ceiling. A clean concrete floor. A few tools on the wall. The light, dim and industrial. Together, we poured the black earth into the pot. I scooped out a hole.

"This is kind of like a scene in a movie, huh?" I asked.

"Yah, this is the touching part." My sister nestled the roots into the soil.

"Two sisters, bent over a plant, lovingly—"

"This is the part in the story where everyone cries."

We started giggling, the kind of giggles we got when we were kids, the kind our parents never understood. Together, we patted down the soil.

I ran to the kitchen for a pitcher to give the plant a drink. It looked a little disheveled, but re-oriented.

"Think they'll feel a little guilty when they see it?" my sister asked.

"I don't know." I held the pot up. "Probably not."

We laughed. She grabbed it, too, and nestled close to me, dramatically, as if we'd been directed to hold that position as the lights dimmed for the closing of the scene.

At the beginning of August, I dreamed I'd killed Jim. I asked my sister to help me hide the body in the master bedroom closet. He kept falling forward and nudging the door open. The police were coming; they were going to search the house. They were sure to find him.

My nightgown is soaked through and I slow to a trot. My feet and calves feel tender. But I don't want to think about turning around, opening that front door, and walking back into my life. And I don't want to think about the questions now bubbling to the surface: Why am I surprised Jim's violence has spilled over onto me? Has my denial been so complete? Do I believe my virtue has somehow protected me? In turn, do I believe my mother is not virtuous enough? Why haven't I tried to stop Jim from hurting her? Am I so desperate for male approval, even from a man I barely know, that I'll sacrifice my mother for it? Am I so self-centered that I can't see violence as fully real until it touches me? The answers suggest a more complicated story, subplots in which I, too, can be implicated. It's too painful to hold the questions long enough to find an answer, so I push them all back under.

I don't know if this is a true memory. It was our last winter in Boulder. In the middle of the night, Jim shook me.

I stirred, groggy, lingering wisps from my dream confusing me.
"I'm on road crew. Wanna come?"
I lifted my head and squinted.
"You said you wanted to come. Snow removal."
I couldn't get my heavy-warm legs to stir. The images from my dream wrapped around me, tugged me back to its watery reality. It was a school night. My head fell to the pillow.
"Are you sure? You said you wanted to come."
I turned over, closed my eyes, and disappeared into my dream.
When I awoke in the morning, I was sorry to have missed a snowy night and felt I'd betrayed Jim. I never told him my regret, and he never asked me to join him again.

I slow to a walk. On the other side of the street is a small church—a worn, '70s-suburban thing with pokey angles—but it has a large overhang at the entrance. I long to feel a divine presence but am embarrassed to think I might find it there: I don't believe God prefers churches over other places—and certainly not such ugly ones. But I cross the street anyway and sit against the front door. The concrete chills my tailbone. My feet sting. Water drips behind my ears and down my neck. I shiver and lift the hem of my nightgown to touch the muddy spots.

I'll write about this someday, I think. But even at fifteen I am embarrassed by how contrived the scene seems: a girl almost hit by her stepfather runs away in the rain in her nightgown and finds comfort under the overhang of a closed church. A cliché from the bad TV movies my mother has taken to watching weekday nights when she's too depressed to move.

The rain falls in silver streaks in the pale orange circle of the streetlight. It drums and splashes, pitters and gurgles. Rain on the roof, rain on the sidewalk, rain on the grass, rain tumbling down drain pipes, rain blown by wind, heavy rain in the distance moving closer. My breathing slows. The edges of the church overhang, the sidewalks, and the sleeping houses seem crisp and distinct, beautifully clean. The streaks of rain have become silver necklaces, chains of miniature diamonds.

My body feels empty, released from cold and fear, full of black space. Then I sense her—that quiet self at my hidden center. The one who is ageless and invisible. Untouched by guilt or betrayal, by rain or fists or shattered flowerpots. What you think is your life, she seems to say, is just a story, the book I read from my quiet, dry place.

Now, years later, I try to recreate that moment at the church with a description of clear edges, rain that looks like jewels, and sudden emptiness. But the words pale, shutters too small to cover the windows.

In the decades after my mother's divorce, I rarely thought of Jim. "He wasn't my real dad," I shrugged when anyone asked. "They were only married for two years. I was already in high school." I don't know why I tell the story now—why the tectonic plates of my interior suddenly shift and thrust to the surface long-buried memories, like dinosaur bones. How do I assemble these bones to tell a true story?

When I open the front door, Jim is gone. I assume my mother has been worried about me, that she will be outraged at Jim. But she sits on her bed, smoking and watching TV, and doesn't seem surprised when I walk in, late and wet, and tell her that Jim tried to hit me. She watches her show and refuses to be angry.

I leave my mother to her cigarettes and TV and float back to my room and book and the sound of the rain. It's okay my mother doesn't want to hear: I couldn't have told her the full story anyway. If I talked about the church, the moment might lose the clear, clean, silver impression in my mind. Even then I knew—to tell a story too soon is to lose it forever.

In Praise of Inadequate Gifts

WHATEVER GETS YOU THROUGH THE NIGHT

You have to do what you do to take care of you.
It ain't wrong if it makes you feel right.
Whatever gets you through the night.

Etta James

My former-hippie mother never imagined she'd end up here: a single mom with two teenage daughters, living in a cheap, suburban house in a military town run by fundamentalist Christians. She'd dreamed of settling into a funky 1930s bungalow in her hometown of Boulder, with hardwood floors and window nooks and a garden. Yet here we were, marooned in a split tri-level, the same model as every third house in our tract, one-third of the way up an enormous, treeless hill.

Two years earlier, my mother and Jim had married, and in a last-ditch effort to save their marriage and finances, we'd crash-landed in Colorado Springs, where the rents were cheap and both she and Jim could find work. But just months after our move, after increasingly violent, police-summoned arguments, Jim left for good, hauling most of our possessions with him.

My mother loved the song "Whatever Gets You Through the Night" by soul singer Etta James. I liked the song's danceable sound and the power and sass in Etta's voice, but her message worried me: A cigarette, a bottle of wine, a walk along a lonely street looking for a man "ain't wrong if it makes you feel right." I appreciated Etta's non-judgmental attitude, but my mother's cigarettes were turning her face gray; Jim's six-packs had twisted him to violence; and some of my parents' old hippie friends, brains fuzzed on drugs, could no longer carry on a coherent conversation. And now my mother spent large swaths of days lying in bed with the shades drawn. Whatever gets you

In Praise of Inadequate Gifts

through the night, if you asked me, was not—as the Beatles said later in the song of the same name— "all right."

In the beginning, after Jim left, this was how my mother made it through the night. She scrubbed the house from top to bottom, as if trying to scrape out every molecule of him. She dragged what remained of our furniture to the family room. There, she tucked my childhood captain's bed into a nook as a reading area and settled a bookshelf next to it. She balanced our old TV and a lopsided plant on top of a wicker trunk. She pushed and tugged our ragged couch and armchair into position. This, of course, left our living room—for most of our neighbors, the showcase into which our front doors opened—empty. At least she'd wrestled one room in our house into coziness.

This is how my eighth-grade sister and I made it through the night. We redefined that empty room. Instead of seeing it as a symbol of all that had gone wrong in our mother's marriages, the physical manifestation of what was empty and lost and ugly, we would see the room as funny. Unexpected. A little quirky rebellion in our neighborhood of cookie cutter houses. And I did like the openness, the way the light poured in the window and bounced off the white walls. Simplicity. Possibility. It was the fall of 1983, the height of the aerobics craze and Jane Fonda exercise videos, so we named the space "the aerobics room." When my sister and I needed a break from our homework or chores, we would do a spontaneous dance, somersault a few times, or do a handstand against the bare wall.

My mother, on the other hand, found our cheerful reframing suspect. That empty room was nothing more than evidence that her ex-husband was an ass. Her life was a series of ever-increasing disappointments, starting with the death of her father when she was seven, reinforced by the crash of her youthful hippie idealism that we could end war and racism, and solidified by the various betrayals of her ex-husbands. And, although she never spoke of it, the rape also must have battered her sense of safety and control. Here she was, barely scraping by, having accomplished nothing of note. My mother

In Praise of Inadequate Gifts

believed our best chance at self-protection was an expectation of the worst and a strong dose of rage.

Here is how I made it through the night. Ambition, compartmentalization, stubborn optimism, and sheer will. I locked my mother's sadness in our house, and as soon as I closed the door behind me, I set about the business of building my future. Mitchell High School, junior year, was my twelfth school, and, I fervently hoped, my last. In the past, I'd sneak into my new school with as little fuss as possible and slink around the margins until my restless mother moved again. This time, though, last chance, I intended to become an improved version of myself.

I began with my classes. In academically rigorous Boulder, due to my fragmented education, I only qualified for regular classes. In Colorado Springs, I boldly talked my way into the honors track.

Next, athletics. I'd recently started running and had experimented with a few road races, but—besides an ill-fated attempt at junior high soccer and a lifetime of misery in PE—I'd never competed in a sport. I joined the cross-country team.

Finally, a personality overhaul. I'd always been shy and made my best effort to cultivate invisibility. But here was my chance to be different. I smiled. I greeted people. I made it a practice to see the best in everyone. The results were immediate: For the first time, a male friend confided I was the "cute new girl" all the boys were talking about.

My mother, on the other hand, worried about my tendency toward optimism. When I was in fifth grade, my mother had no trouble with me reading her copy of *Rubyfruit Jungle*, a coming-of-age lesbian novel with explicit sex scenes. But she grew agitated when I became mesmerized by *The Sound of Music*, playing on TV one Sunday afternoon. On the way to the kitchen from the bathroom, cleaning rag in her hand, the smell of bleach lingering in the air behind her, my mother slowed, almost stopped, and watched me with that *I don't approve but I don't know if I should say anything* tightness in her face.

The music was a problem—that I immediately understood. My

mother listened mostly to old soul and blues, occasionally some bluegrass or 70s funk, but nothing by overly cheerful white girls. She wanted some grit, some depth, some suffering in her voices. And she didn't like the artificialness of those choreographed dance moves. Later, my fondness for *The Sound of Music* would become a family joke, and my sister and mother would tease me for my insipid taste, but now I believe there was another dimension I sensed then, but didn't yet understand: My mother was disturbed by a character who faced the horrors of the incipient Holocaust by singing "raindrops on roses and whiskers on kittens." She wanted to stamp the Julie Andrews out of me.

After Jim left, my mother was no longer doing a very good job of making it through the night. Some days she couldn't make it to her paralegal job. She'd spend all day in her graying robe, chain-smoking on her bed or sitting on the bottom of the stairs, staring into the aerobics room. If she could find the energy, she'd cry. Sometimes she'd rant, beginning with my stepfather, circling back to my father, whom she'd left long ago, then spiraling back to her family who had never known how to give her what she needed.

Here's how my sister and I made it through the night. We found boyfriends. Tim was a senior who lived across the street. I'd noticed him driving his yellow and black Datsun, small and pointed like a yellow jacket. I usually fell for slight, artistic boys, but Tim looked like an all-American football player. A wide, healthy smile. Brown hair with auburn highlights. And already a man's body, with broad shoulders. I fantasized that, like teenagers I'd seen in movies, I'd date a football player. First, Tim and I gave each other lingering looks across our lawns, and then after our first awkward introduction, he offered to drive my sister and me to school. Because Tim's brother sat in the front, I sat in the back and kept catching Tim's copper-colored eyes in the rearview mirror. And then he was my boyfriend. He wasn't a football player. He was a soccer player, which was cool enough in our school, and he played the French horn in the band, which wasn't, but I didn't mind. He was devoted and attentive and stabilizing,

In Praise of Inadequate Gifts

which I needed more than I realized.

We hung out in the aerobics room. On our hands and knees, we played hand soccer, batting a piece of balled-up paper into makeshift goals. But really, it was an opportunity to bump against each other as often as possible.

Tim's little brother David, a sophomore, developed a crush on my sister, and soon they were a couple. So the aerobics room was theirs, too. They sat on the floor and leaned against the wall, nuzzling their noses into each other's necks, cuddling their joint teddy bear, and calling each other pet names in baby voices. In the evenings, my sister and I took turns stretching the phone cord from the kitchen around the corner to the aerobics room for private conversations with our boyfriends.

But Tim and David's father, Mr. Brown, did not want his sons speaking with us on the phone or wandering over to our yard in the afternoons and evenings. I'd later learn Mr. Brown was Polish and had grown up in New York, the son of a waitress. He'd almost gone to seminary to become a priest, but had instead married a beautiful woman from Puerto Rico, had five children, and became an administrator in a school for teenagers with behavior problems. But at the time, I knew only that he didn't like me and I didn't know why.

I begged Tim to explain.

"Your mother's divorced . . ."

That was the first time I'd run into explicit prejudice against divorced women. "Yes?" I asked pointedly.

"And . . . well . . . you're all blonde."

I didn't understand. "Yes?"

"So, you know . . ."

I guess Mr. Brown did not think I was Julie Andrews.

Tim thought I was too much like Julie Andrews. After we'd been together several months, we had a fight. Tim thought I smiled too freely at school. We tried to work it out on the phone. This time I stood in the kitchen, around the corner from the aerobics room, so my voice wouldn't float up the stairs and wake my mother and sister. Tim stated his central complaint: "You're so nice. You smile at everyone. How am I supposed to know you love me best? You're supposed to love me the most."

I don't remember the details of the rest of the conversation, but I know this: I was pained I'd hurt Tim. But I also didn't want to make myself smaller. And it was too late at night. We'd talked for too long. We were debriefing our debriefing, and I was long past my rational hour. I sank to the floor and lay my forehead on the cold linoleum. His words were buzzing bees. I'd lost all the spiraling threads of our conversation and had decided I didn't know anything about anything. But then he said something I've never forgotten: "I want in," he said. "You only let me in so far. I want all of you." And suddenly, I saw he was right.

This is how I made it through the night. I had an empty room inside me. I had never consciously considered it before, but instantly I had an image of my interior room: a long oval that filled my torso from my collar bone to my hips, windowless, empty of furniture, empty of anything but safety and stillness. I'd first learned to retreat into that room during the series of small apartments, where I'd lived with my mother and sister, filled with loud music, TV, and talk—often all at once. My interior room was the only reliably quiet place. And as much as I'd trained myself to be more outgoing, I was still shy about allowing long-term guests in my interior room. But I did have visitors. The occasional close friend. Tim. Over and over, my mother had knocked, and I had let her in and then regretted it—as she had a habit, when her darkness descended again, of turning what my sister and I shared in intimate moments against us.

As a result, in the upper right of the oval was a room within a room, only a box really, which I thought was invisible, which belonged only to me. No one else, no matter how close, could enter. But Tim had glimpsed my box—which surprised me, as I hardly knew it existed myself—and he was knocking. Asking for unlimited access. Whether or not love meant opening that box I didn't know, but fierce invisible dogs, panicked dogs, protected the lock, and I had no power to tame them.

This is how my mother made it through the night: She'd rage at my

In Praise of Inadequate Gifts

sister and me for all we couldn't do for her. She believed we didn't recognize the gravity of her situation, her loneliness and financial strain. Instead of keeping her company, we spent time with our boyfriends and did our homework. We harassed her with requests for rides to our jobs or reminders we were out of food, as if she weren't trying to swim though a tar pit all by herself.

"You God damn fucking bitch," she would yell at one of us, when she was particularly exasperated with our self-absorption.

This is how my sister and I made it through the night. We turned our mother's favorite phrase into an acronym: GDFB.

"How was your day, GDFB?"

"Just fine; how was yours, GDFB?"

Then we'd laugh.

Not long before my stepfather left, taking the furniture with him, my mother sat at the bottom of the stairs, in her faded, grimy nightgown, staring into what would soon be the empty room. Her pretty blonde hair, which usually received too much of her attention, was matted on one side, sticking up on the other. Her face was pasty gray. Her eyes were puffy from crying, and without mascara, her eyelashes disappeared. Her bare feet looked bloated, a little red and raw.

I'd become practiced at soothing her: Make her coffee. Rub her back. Stop my homework to watch TV with her. Listen to her while she cried. Sleep in her bed when she asked—even though I didn't like the cigarette smell of the room; the way the TV in her room blared all night; her scratchy legs pressed against mine; the way I had to slip into the crack between the bed and wall to find any space at all.

My mother had tipped over some edge from hopelessness into something closer to illness. She obsessed over the smallest slights from friends, relatives, co-workers. She told and retold a real or imagined injustice until it ballooned in her mind and she was filled with rage. Then she might end a lifelong friendship, cut off another family member, tell off her boss, quit her job again. Sometimes, if I said just the right thing at just the right time—the perfect balance between acknowledging her feelings and herding her reasoning in a more

In Praise of Inadequate Gifts

rational direction—I could dissipate, at least for a while, the gathering storm. I was successful just often enough to convince me my job was essential.

However, at that moment at the bottom of the stairs, I knew by the way my mother sucked fast and angry on her cigarette, the time for a successful intervention had passed. A fresh and irresistible surge of anger was building under her silence. If I spoke, I could unleash it. If I ignored her, I could unleash it. So I tried to float through the house like a phantom, doing some cleaning I hoped would placate her.

She breathed, "I'm going to have to leave him . . ."

I stopped, cleaning rag in my hand. I knew that could mean another move, another town. My carefully constructed life: my boyfriend, my classes, my cross-country team, all began to teeter, then slowly evaporate, as if they'd been an illusion all along. I don't remember what I told her, only that I used all my skills. My voice was calm, full of affection. And when her anger eased a little, I began to edge her toward giving her marriage another chance. But as soon as she recognized I had an agenda, her eyes hardened.

"Look at me," she said. Slowly. Firmly.

Gray face and hands. Gray-blue eyes, now sharp. Round red toes. A nightgown, open at the neck, exposing her graceful collarbones.

Then louder. Tense and angry. "Look at me!" She shook her fingers at her jaw line.

Then I saw. An enormous, purple lump of a bruise. Thumbprints of yellow and green around the edges.

When she knew she had my attention, and I couldn't speak for shock, her anger drained. "He knocked my molar loose." She turned toward the wall and began to cry. "I don't have the money to get it fixed."

I was horrified. I had made it through the night by being blind to a bruise the size of a tennis ball. I was so concerned about preserving the life I'd crafted, I hadn't seen what was right in front of me. Here was the dark underside of optimism. Here was the danger of my interior room, where, it now appeared, I could create my own alternate reality, where optimism could morph into delusion.

Then I almost didn't make it through the night. About six months after my stepfather left, my mother again sat on the stairs in that same nightgown, the ashtray overflowing beside her, staring into the empty room.

"I can't do it. I just can't do it." She began to cry.

This time, I sat on the carpet below her, arms around my knees, brainstorming about finances, offering to get a second job, assuring her of her resilience. Slowly, as I talked, the tension eased from her face and shoulders. But then her body tightened again and her eyes got hard and flat. "I'm going to have to send you to your father's. There's no other way."

My thoughts, which had been wrapped around her, tumbled back on myself. Exhaustion at the thought of another move, this time to my father's less familiar chaos in Canada. Grief at saying goodbye, not only to my new life, but to Colorado sunshine and pine trees and wide blue skies. Fear that another academic interruption, another country, could be a dangerous detour on my route to college. Worst of all, under those fears, a slow dawning awareness that perhaps my mother didn't intend to send me away, but was just trying to hurt me. Because she needed her hurt to be my hurt, too.

I rolled over on my side in a ball and squeezed my eyes shut. My thoughts raced into a senseless blur and then blanked. I tried to pull into my interior room, but the walls disintegrated and the space was flooded with a gray, blinding light. In my imagination, I saw myself spread out on my back on the floor. I was melting. I was melting into the carpet. My mother kept talking, her anger building. But I couldn't hear her. My skin melted, then, one by one, my organs melted, until all that was left was a beating heart. Then it, too, melted, this time into a small ball of mercury, silver and strange. She talked and her words were another language.

Then I was big again. And my insides were being scooped out. Scooped out with a big spoon. All that was left was a shell. The shell was green and dry and crispy. A grasshopper shell. Her words were a black background hum. And then I saw a black hole. I was spiraling into the hole, spiraling, spiraling into nothingness. I sensed I was about to cross a boundary from which I might not return into light or language. I'd passed the place where will or fierce hope could help. Then a voice from the expansive darkness.

"Tarn."

My mother's voice. Firm. Clear. Sure.

"Tarn, come back. Come back."

I was spiraling, but I found, deeper than I knew I could reach, enough strength to pull myself from the spiraling, sucking hole that promised rest and oblivion. I followed the voice. I fought my way back to the floor, my body, my arms around my knees.

The next day, in the kitchen, I said shyly to my mother, who was subdued, making her coffee, getting out the ironing board to ready her clothes for work, "Thank you. For yesterday."

She looked puzzled.

"For calling me back."

She still looked puzzled.

"When I was on the floor."

She didn't know what I was talking about.

Something had called me back. A voice disguised. Maybe some deep part of myself I'd never met. Maybe God. This was a different God than the one I thought I knew, who loved me only when I was cheerful and good. This God reached for me when I was a dried husk, a ball of mercury. This was a God who could help me make it through the night.

Several months later, around seven in the evening, the doorbell rang. I opened the front door to find Mr. Brown, Tim's father, standing there. He was a stocky man with sloped shoulders, a pronounced nose, and a wide mouth. And a grim expression.

"Hi, Mr. Brown!" I smiled broadly and tried to look wholesome.

The empty room behind me, my happy room for cartwheels and kisses, suddenly seemed the sign of a family in which something was seriously amiss.

In Praise of Inadequate Gifts

He looked at me sternly. "I'd like to talk to your mother."

Guilt washed over me. I wasn't sure what I'd done. But, having recently discovered the pleasure of new and longer kinds of kisses, I felt guilty most of the time. Maybe I *was* what Mr. Brown feared.

"Janet . . ." I called down to the family room where she was sitting in her brown chair, feet up on the ottoman. Then I remembered most people don't call their mothers by their first names, as my sister and I always had. That didn't look good either.

"Mum . . ." I'd taken to calling her that occasionally in sixth grade when she and I had both become obsessed with British mini-series on public television.

"Who is it?" she called back, half-curious, half-irritated to be bothered.

I leaned around the corner and called down to her. "Mr. Brown wants to talk to you."

She pulled on her skirt over her slip, straightened her shirt, kicked her balled up nylons under the chair, and walked up the stairs in her bare feet.

"Hi, Mr. Brown."

We called all our other neighbors by their first names, including Mr. Brown's wife, Wanda. But Mr. Brown was Mr. Brown. Even to my mother.

"We need to talk."

"Okay," she said, a little defensiveness in her voice. I stood behind her right shoulder.

He looked pointedly at me. "Privately."

My mother paused. I could feel animal protectiveness rising in her. But she couldn't figure out how to say no to Mr. Brown. She looked at me.

I turned and bound up the stairs, two at a time, to the upper floor, where I pressed myself against the wall where they couldn't see me.

"My niece, Tim's older cousin . . . driving past Denny's . . . saw my son and your daughter eating pancakes . . . during school hours. Called me right away. I called the high school . . . your

In Praise of Inadequate Gifts

daughter was absent during seventh period."

Seventh period. Seventh period. Art. I was late. I'd been working with student council. My teacher must have marked me absent instead of tardy. I wanted to leap down the stairs to defend myself, but I couldn't give away I'd been listening.

"As the *adults* in the neighborhood"—he emphasized the word *adults* as if to convince my mother she needed to be more of one—"we need to work together to . . ."

I wasn't afraid my mother would punish me—long lectures in which I was made to feel guilty for my selfishness was the extent of her discipline—but I didn't want her to believe something false about me.

I strained to hear my mother's response:

"I hope it's true." She spoke with a voice full of emotion. "She's always been the most responsible person I know—since she was a little girl. She works so hard. She takes care of *me*. I'd be happy, for once, if she let herself have a little fun."

Mr. Brown was too surprised to answer.

(Later, he would change his mind about us and we would all become honorary family members at his bustling dinner table. Sometimes, your neighbors can help you make it through the night. But that was yet to come.)

My mother turned all her force on Mr. Brown. "Didn't you have fun in high school?"

I released a breath I felt I'd been holding most of my life. Tears welled in my eyes.

I heard the front door close.

In just a moment, I would step down the stairs and into our empty aerobics room and my mother would tell the story and roll her eyes at Mr. Brown.

But for now, I wanted one more moment feeling that unfamiliar openness in my chest. My mother wanted more for me. In her best moments, she wanted more for me than she could give me and more than I could give myself. More freedom. More fun. More self-acceptance. Neither of us knew how to be different. Neither of us

In Praise of Inadequate Gifts

had figured out healthy ways to make it through the night. But she wanted more for me.

DISASTER MAN

My mother's date stood on our front walkway, a late Friday afternoon, under the flat, brilliant blue Denver sky. His sports coat hung over his arm. I was in sixth grade, and I'd never met a man who wore a business shirt—or cologne. When he moved his jacket from one arm to the other, he released a smell: cloves with a hint of flowers.

Usually on Friday nights, my mother, sister, and I ate buttered popcorn out of a big bowl and watched *Love Boat* and *Fantasy Island*. Our mother lounged in her brown recliner chair in her slip and work shirt, recovering from the week. My sister and I were required to take turns rubbing her back and shoulders. "Oh, your little hands. They can just get right in there and get out all those knots." Her praise made us proud—it was nice to be good at something grown up, like massage—but her sighs of release carried a longing for closeness we didn't want to meet. We wanted instead to be lying on the floor on our stomachs watching attractive people have romantic misadventures in tropical settings.

My mother thought the storylines were ridiculous, and if she wasn't too tired, she'd groan, "Oh, brother," at some particularly corny scene and roll her eyes. She was very good at eye rolling.

"Yah. *Stupid*," my sister and I'd echo. We wanted to be sophisticated for a fourth and a sixth grader. We wouldn't fall for any ridiculous fantasy.

My mother hadn't been out with a man since we'd moved to Colorado, three years before. There'd been Carl, of course, but he didn't count. She'd loved him long before we were born, before my father, and he showed up every few years or so, stayed a few days, and left. We loved him, my little sister and I, but knew he wouldn't stay. Carl. Who was short and sturdy and had gray speckles in his hair and played blues piano and listened to us as if we were as smart and interesting as grownups. But my mother said "Good morning!" in too perky a way: Jewish women never said good morning like that, he said. It was a symbol of all their differences that couldn't be bridged. Carl wouldn't keep her, but it would be a long time before he finally let her go.

We came from five generations of female-only families. I knew the most recent stories: My great-grandfather abandoned his family, and my grandmother was raised by her mother, grandmother, and aunt. My grandfather died when my mother was seven, and she was raised by her mother and two older sisters. "It's a curse," my grandmother told my mother in her Southern accent. "The women in our family always lose our men."

My mother was bitter after her divorce and, fed by the feminism of the seventies, refused to say being man-less was a curse. Really, men were the problem. Simone De Beauvoir's *The Second Sex* sat on her bookshelf next to angry, inspiring books by Black women. My mother intended to reinvent the family story: we were three strong women against the world.

So my sister and I knew we should hide our attraction to TV romance. When the couples finally got together, we kept our happy sighs to ourselves.

I don't remember where our mother first met her date—the oil company where she was a manager or the Italian bar where she sometimes hung out with her new group of friends—but she told us about him nonchalantly.

"This guy asked me out." We were in the kitchen eating from the bowl of homemade frosting my sister concocted every afternoon for a snack.

"Who is it? Do you like him? Are you going to go?" Real life romance! My aunt, who was a model, had shown our mother how to wear make-up, and she'd bought some high-heeled shoes, so now she was pretty in a TV way.

"I don't know . . ." She absently put the spoon in her mouth. "He's a doctor . . ."

As a sixth grader, I was astute enough to know that her date's profession—a selling point for most women—was a complication for my mother. She was not many years from her hippie-life with my father. She now curled her blonde hair and wore tan skirts to the office, but she could at least claim that she was a struggling single mother—there was some working-class dignity in that. To date—and perhaps marry—a doctor would please her Southern belle mother and sisters too much, might make a mockery of her years as a socialist, an anti-war activist, a woman living off the land with my father in the Canadian wilderness.

"Go. You have to go," we said. We couldn't help ourselves. We'd transformed into social directors on the *Love Boat*.

"Maybe." She looked at the frosting on the tip of her spoon and then put it in her mouth.

Secretly, although we never confessed it to each other, my sister and I also wanted a dad. We visited our father in the summers, but he wasn't the kind of dad who called in the off-season. We wanted someone who could toss us around, wrestle, teach us to throw a ball so we wouldn't be so embarrassed in PE. Someone who would make us laugh. Someone who would make our mother feel safe.

And I liked that he was a doctor, although I'd never tell my mother. She'd think I was superficial. But people think doctors are important, and an important person thought my mother was attractive. And, although I wouldn't let my imagination wander too far down this path—I didn't want to hope too much or be one of the bourgeoisie my parents taught me to despise—I wondered, for a moment, what it would be like to have enough money. We'd have food all the way till the end of the month.

My mother needed more time to dress, so she ushered my sister and me out the door to entertain her date in the front yard. We—who had been noisy-wild in anticipation of his arrival—were suddenly made mute by the reality of him: his jacket and white shirt and clove smell and his awkward shifting in his polished black shoes.

He asked us a few questions, the kind a single man in his thirties knows to ask elementary school girls.

"How old are you? "

In Praise of Inadequate Gifts

We'd watched enough TV movies to know that, for a single woman, children were a liability. And we were what some people might call "a handful." At the mall, we ran up the down escalators and down the up escalators; in the public bathrooms, we locked all the stalls and then crawled under the doors; in the department store, we stood frozen in the display windows pretending we were manikins until a crowd gathered—and we saw our mother's weary face gesturing us to come home. We thought it best to hide our true natures. But what did polite, good children talk about? We didn't know. So we stood up straight and gave one-word answers.

"Eleven." "Nine."

"What grades are you in?"

His face was smooth. Neat and clean. Maybe too clean, for my mother. He wasn't a Marlborough Man; instead of a cowboy hat on his head, he had a bald spot in the middle of his otherwise perfect black hair.

Although my mother hadn't dated in years, she had slept with the man across the street and two houses down. My sister had found them in bed together, but closed the door before they saw her, and she'd carried this secret for months before she blurted it out when we were doing our chores together.

I didn't ask my sister why she hadn't told me earlier. I knew. Our mother didn't love the man and that fact would have embarrassed her. Sure, he was a nice guy. Sturdy. Blonde. A surfer dude without the water. Cheerful. But he wasn't too smart. Once, he had invited us all to his bachelor pad, where we sat stiffly on his white leather couch and listened to him explain the finer points of his new sound system. Worst of all, he listened to the Beach Boys. "I'm pickin' up good vibrations" blasted down the block. That was fine by me—it seemed the sort of song a sixth-grade girl should have in the background while skipping down the sidewalk—but my mother listened only to soul music. Black women with attitude. Aretha Franklin. The Pointer Sisters. Sister Sledge. Music that had depth, that could hold suffering. The Beach Boys were close to sin. Pure loneliness had driven my mother into his arms. That's what my sister

In Praise of Inadequate Gifts

was protecting: that vulnerability at her center.

"Do you like school?"

My sister told him about the report she'd written on pygmy marmosets while I decided I liked his bald spot. A fit doctor with clear skin and a fine nose could easily be proud. But I guessed his bald spot kept him humble, and that kind of humility, I'd learned, usually led to kindness.

"What's your favorite subject?"

He'd run out of questions. Shifted. Moved his jacket, again, from one arm to the other. Looked at the sky. At our faces, smiled briefly. Looked at the lawn across the street. Then his face lit up, and we turned to see our mother walking toward us.

I don't remember what she wore. Her black leotard and Indian skirt, maybe. Or something more modest, but still sexy: an A-lined skirt and her high-heeled Candies. I do know that her blonde hair was smooth and curled and she was beautiful and a man was waiting for her.

My mother saw our conversation had stalled, so she interjected a starter: "He was in an airplane crash."

This of course was thrilling news, and my sister and I forgot to be polite and wanted to know every detail. How big was the plane? Did he think he was going to die? Was he afraid? Yes, he said, a little. Did the airplane start on fire? How were they rescued? I've since forgotten most of his answers, but not the new, jaunty expression on his face.

"I was in a tornado, too."

We were suitably impressed. "Was it just like in *The Wizard of Oz*? Did it pick you up off the ground? Were you whirled around?"

His arms came alive as he answered.

"Have you been in a tidal wave?" my sister asked, her body tight with excitement.

"Actually, yes, I have. I was in Hawaii . . ." The way his voice got lower, more self-important and authoritative, made me think he was embellishing. But I didn't mind. I liked a good story. Besides, that showed he wanted to impress us, which meant he probably had a

In Praise of Inadequate Gifts

genuine interest in our mother. Maybe my mother was imagining traveling there. A tropical setting.

"Have you been in a forest fire?" my sister asked, mesmerized.

"A fire, yes, but it was a building fire, not a forest . . ."

That was a good move. A yes to every question might look as if he were lying.

But my mother wasn't asking any questions. She was glancing down the street, as if bored. Her lips were in a line.

Suddenly I realized that a man who wants to attract a woman probably shouldn't describe himself as a natural disaster magnet. And he was talking too much. The *Love Boat* director in me wanted to pull him aside and whisper some tips: Change the subject. Look at her. Don't talk so long. Ask her some questions.

"Have you been in an avalanche?" my sister was having fun now, searching her brain for disaster vocabulary words.

"Yes!" he said, as if surprised himself by the growing list. "We were skiing in Aspen . . ."

I saw a sigh escape from my mother's chest.

"An earthquake?"

"A little one."

"Was there a big crack in the ground and did you fall in?"

"No," he laughed and he didn't have time to elaborate because the babysitter's car was at the corner and my sister wanted to insert as many disasters as she could before they had to leave. "A boat accident?"

"No."

And then my mother's friend Barb was beside us. She must have been playing *Love Boat* director, too, because she'd never babysat for us before and certainly not on a Friday night, when she could be out with her new boyfriend. We all admired Barb's new perm, and then Disaster Man touched my mother's elbow to guide her toward the car. Barb ushered us toward the house where we would, in a couple of hours, eat popcorn and watch the *Love Boat* and *Fantasy Island* and wonder if my mother was having fun on her date.

The next day, as usual, my mother slept in and my sister and I spent a typical Saturday morning on the floor in front of the TV in our pajamas, eating Cheerios and watching cartoons, first the shows we liked and then, as the morning rolled on, the ones we didn't. By noon, the TV had sucked all the energy right out of us, and we were grouchy and greasy-feeling. Cereal bowls and spoons and couch cushions littered the floor. In her rumpled nightgown, my mother finally stumbled from her bed and to the kitchen, where she started the coffee maker. We followed.

We asked her about her date. I don't know how she responded. Two pseudo-memories seem equally true: she was withdrawn and non-committal, or she made merciless fun of him. I do know she chose not to go out with him again or, for a long while, any man.

In the weeks after that date, my sister and I recreated our conversation with the doctor over and over reciting his list of disasters.

My mother would roll her eyes: "Oh, God, wasn't that weird? He talked about them like he was proud or something. And 'when I was in *Aspen* . . .when I was in *Hawaii*' . . . what a show off."

Soon, in our family lore, her date would evolve from a real man with a real name into Disaster Man. A joke of a name. A name that made us feel superior. My sister still felt compelled to list the disasters, vicariously experiencing the adrenaline rush that comes from impending bodily harm. "First there was the airplane crash. An avalanche. A tidal wave. And what's the difference between a hurricane and a tornado? Was he in both?"

I thought of the way he moved his arms as he talked, how much he wanted to impress us, the gentle, formal way he held my mother's elbow. If he were on the *Love Boat*, he could have won her.

"And the house fire, but not a forest fire. Do you think he's been struck by lightning? . . ." and then my sister's words trailed off, as she'd realized she'd never get to ask.

But who was I to choose for my mother? Even then I knew attraction was a mystery. And I wanted to believe my mother, that he was awkward and unworthy of her. At the same time, I feared that her fears and doubts had dressed themselves in standards so narrow

In Praise of Inadequate Gifts

she'd never love again. She wouldn't find a father for me, nor the companion I'd hoped for her: someone to rub the knots out her back and answer her sighs.

I also had my own sense of unease about Disaster Man. What were the chances that one man had experienced so much danger? It seemed to defy the odds. What, then, was the cause? Was there something in his thinking that attracted disasters? Something in disasters that drew him to them? Was he cursed?

"Quicksand," my sister muttered. "I should have asked him about quicksand."

Several years later, when I was in junior high school, my mother did marry again, a cowboy paving contractor, a Marlborough Man. She had fallen for her own fantasy, and it was a disaster of a relationship. She was disappointed in all he couldn't be; his drinking escalated along with her screaming. He beat her then almost killed her. The marriage lasted two years. For the rest of her life, she never loved another man

II.

HIDE AND SEEK WITH THE DEAD

You didn't believe in life after death, but I think you visited me the night you died.

You'd been ill for seven years, such a long stretch beyond the few years the doctors had granted you. So when my sister Rima called to say she thought you were dying, I wasn't ready. I raced to book the early morning flight from California to British Columbia and finish the work necessary to exit life-as-I-knew it: find teachers to cover my classes, throw substitute plans together, cancel appointments, pack.

Around nine that night, most of the tasks done, I entered the bathroom, tight with fear and exhaustion. I'd just finished peeing and was pulling up my jeans when I heard your voice. Loud. Clear. Unmistakably you.

One short sentence that muted all the other chatter in my mind. "I'm okay," you said.

I breathed—I hadn't noticed I'd been holding my breath—and felt the tension drain from my body. You were okay. You weren't dying after all. My sister had misunderstood.

When I could hear my own thoughts again, I was suddenly embarrassed: You'd come to speak to me and I'd been peeing! Then I felt you say, this time not in a clear sentence, more a feeling, but an unmistakable message: "Don't be ridiculous. I took care of you when you were small. I changed your diapers. I bathed you. . ." From you, my former-hippie father who thought I was too proper, this comment was part rebuke, part comfort, part laughing at me.

And then you were gone.

By the time I arrived in Canada, you'd already died, probably around four in the morning. My sister said you'd slipped into a coma at nine the night before, the very moment you'd spoken to me in the bathroom. I told my sister about the timing of your visit, and we stared at each other, speechless.

When I was a child, I wanted to be as smart and scientific as you. I believed, and was happy to tell anyone who asked: "When you're dead, you're dead. You're in the ground and that's that." I was mature, able to face the facts better than grownups.

I don't know when exactly my beliefs started to change, or why, but by the time I was in the middle of my teenage years, I was certain of continued existence—I couldn't say what that existence might be, but I felt surer of it than some of the facts in my textbooks.

Toward the end of college, long before anyone I loved had died, I was obsessed by books about life-after-death experiences. Stories of those who floated peacefully above their bodies while doctors tried to resuscitate them and relatives held their hands. Sometimes, the dead would think of someone they loved, and, regardless of distance, instantly appear by their side. Most saw a tunnel with a white light at the end. Some passed through waves of exquisite music or fields of wildflowers. When they reached the light, some saw a figure they thought was Jesus. Others were bathed in warmth and love. Most returned with the same message: The purpose of life is to love and to learn. Yes, I was embarrassed by the cheesy book covers with glowing angels—and suspicious of writers who seemed to have a hidden, denominational agenda—but still, I couldn't stop reading.

Once, I shared some stories with you. Trained as a mathematician and scientist, you didn't deny the experiences must have *felt* real, but they were, you insisted, merely the pyrotechnics of a dying brain. I told you a story about a man who'd gone into a coma and died. He'd floated above his body and then down the hallway, where he listened to the doctors talking below him. When he was resuscitated, he reported exact lines of their conversation, and even described the clothes the doctors were wearing.

You paused. The writer, you said, was making it up.

I wish I could talk to you about the night you died and the "I'm okay" you spoke in the bathroom. The living you would have laughed at me for creating meaning from coincidence and imagination. I'd argue back that if I were inventing words, I'd have chosen different ones, a longer sentence perhaps. The word *love* in there somewhere. I'd have picked a different time—even twenty seconds later when my pants were up.

In Praise of Inadequate Gifts

I want to disagree with you, but I don't know where to find you.

When I landed in Seattle to change planes, I listened to the phone message telling me you'd died. I called my sister, and after we cried, she asked, "Do you, you know, want to see the body?"

The question surprised me, so I was silent.

She was apologetic, "'Cause I have to tell the people. When they should come get him. Do you want us to wait?"

"No, thank you for asking. But, no."

Her tone was almost desperate: "I needed it, for closure. It's very helpful." She feared I was making a decision I'd regret.

In this airport conversation, with the loud flight announcements in the background, there was no space for conversation about our decisions, about why she wanted to see your body and I didn't. I didn't tell her I'm highly susceptible to images; they burn into me. I didn't want your dead body to be the picture that overrode all my other memories. I didn't think I could find you in your body.

Several months after your cremation, your wife, Prairie, sent me a padded envelope. I assumed it was a memento, some little object you'd loved. I opened a black velvet box to find a pretty pendant on a chain, a small silver canister etched with graceful curlicues. Only when I saw the canister partially twisted open and the dusting of powder against black velvet, did I realize what it was.

Then I saw the note: Prairie and Rima had purchased five pendants—one for Prairie and one for each of your four daughters; you were the link between your far-flung children from three marriages. Maybe Prairie and Rima hoped if we each carried a bit of your body, you'd link us still. To them, those ashes must be, in some form, the man they loved. To me they are like ashes in a fireplace, too far removed from log and fire to hold the shape of you.

What, then, do I do with my pendant? I won't wear it around my neck.

"Nice necklace."

"Thanks, it's my dead dad."

I don't want to hang it on my bulletin board with my other happy souvenirs on strings. For a day, I stored it in my desk drawer, but every time I opened it to get my scissors or stapler, there it was: "Your dad is dead. Dead. Dead. Death. Die. Loss. Disease. Gone gone gone."

But now that it's in the house—like a curmudgeonly stray cat— I can't cast it out.

On my desk I keep a small box with drawers. On the top, I've arranged objects that inspire me. Only now do I recognize that most of them remind me of you. An owl feather, bright marbles, a stuffed meadowlark that sings a meadowlark song when I squeeze him, rocks from the Canadian Island where we lived in my early childhood. A soapstone carving of a Japanese lady a missionary gave to your mother just after WWII, which you presented to me not long before you died. A photograph of me holding a baby in a red dress and a white sunhat, a baby named after me. My goddaughter, Baby Tarn.

You named me. A name that carries what you valued. A mountain lake. A geological term. A crossword puzzle word. Now a baby you have never met carries the name you loved. I see more of you, then, in that name, in that baby's face, than in that black velvet box I finally tuck behind the photograph: still with my special objects, but where I can't see it.

Years ago, when I was in my mid-twenties, we met again after a four-year estrangement. Do you remember? You and my mother had scratched your way through several court cases about back child support, woven with convoluted lies on both sides. I grieved the childhood years we didn't see you and you didn't contact us, the way my sister and I went without so much when you had enough to share. But my longing for you hadn't eased. I lived in California, but that summer I was a counselor at a Canadian camp only a few ferry rides from you. I had a rare day off, so we met on an island in-between, a restaurant on a harbor, overlooking a bay. We'd reserved an afternoon and evening for each other.

I was writing a memoir about my early childhood, and I intended to interview you. Even more, although I wasn't fully aware of it at the time, I wanted to find my way back to you. I didn't know how to begin, so I opened my little journal to ask you questions.

As we ate, I jotted down a few of your memories. Talking about the past made you restless, so halfway through the meal, you changed the subject.

"So, why are you a vegetarian?"

I paused. My decision was largely intuitive, not political or intellectual, so it was hard to translate into words. I smoothed my napkin on my lap. "I think it's a peaceful way to live. I don't like to kill animals . . . I don't like the way animals are treated."

You answered with one of your scientific lectures, the kind I remembered from childhood. "Energy moves in a closed system. When you eat animals, you keep the energy moving through the system. It's necessary."

I thought you were enjoying the conversation, the rub of mind against mind. I thought we were disagreeing for fun, like we did when I was a kid. I mulled over your point.

"That's assuming it's a closed system." I was talking about God, of course. Or whatever name you might give the force from which life and energy might originate. But I would never use that word with you, my atheist father.

You didn't miss the allusion. You raised your voice—you rarely raised your voice—and sputtered, "You can't just say that. You can't just make up the rules. We have to agree on certain basic premises or nobody can talk to anyone!" You yelled and threw up your hands: "You might as well just make up anything you want!"

I was silent, watching you. I'd be hurt and confused later, but then I was only stunned.

You balled up your napkin and threw it on your seat. "I have to go to the bathroom." When you returned, you didn't sit back down: "This dinner is over."

We didn't talk again for several years.

I could understand your argument, but I didn't understand your anger, especially from a man whose emotions were usually so even, and hidden. Were you actually hurt about the years of silence between us? Maybe your anger was less about me and more about your beliefs about women, those former wives who frustrated you with

In Praise of Inadequate Gifts

their lack of logic and big emotions. Did you think my spiritual beliefs had somehow separated me from you? Maybe my interview had agitated you, my probing about those years before my mother left you, asking questions you didn't know how to answer.

Or was it something else I can't guess?

Over time, we cautiously connected again, but I no longer spoke to you of mysteries.

I never told you that before my boss Helen died, the photographs of her on the school wall started glowing. Helen was the counselor and a founder of a small alternative high school where I taught in my twenties. A life-changing mentor. After my first two years in the job, Helen retired. Not long after, we learned she'd been sick, but she'd hidden from the teachers just how ill she was. One afternoon after the students had gone, I walked down the hallway where we'd posted photographs of student activities: a college field trip; a team-building exercise; service projects cleaning a creek and painting over graffiti.

In the photographs, Helen was glowing. All the other faces were two-dimensional, dull, but Helen looked bathed in a spotlight. No, more as if she'd been lit from within. She was carved of light— her lion face, her fuzzy gold hair, her strong arms.

I couldn't tell anyone, "Helen is glowing!" and maintain the appearance of public-school-teacher sanity, so I just stuck my head in the principal's office.

"Is Helen alright?"

The principal looked at me, and I knew she wasn't.

All week, Helen-in-the-photographs glowed for me, startling me every time I passed. And then she died.

After her death, the photographs were dull again.

In the years following our dinner in the restaurant, I learned to give up my efforts to encourage you to talk about your past, hopes, regrets, my childhood, or our relationship. Instead, I'd sit with you in silence and listen, without interruption, to whatever anecdotes you offered. And with my new slowness, you began to tell me stories I'd never heard.

The year before your death, I visited you for a week. On my last night, you offered to take me out to dinner. You were frail by then. For most of my life you'd been a workaholic—most recently in your venture as the owner of a used books/local art/coffee shop—so it was odd to see you working only half days and taking long naps every afternoon. By this time, even one block's walk was difficult, so I felt especially honored you'd asked me to dinner. I thought you might have a message for me.

You dressed up in a dusty tweed jacket. I wore the one skirt I brought, a black T-shirt, and some flip-flops. The Inglenook, a German restaurant, was an old three-story house tucked in a grove of cedars. Our walk to the stairs was slow. I waited for you, the same father who used to race me down the beach, shirtless and in bare feet, then throw me in the air. It was just after five and the restaurant was almost empty. The owners chatted with you—they hadn't seen you around lately. You didn't tell them about your illness. You asked them to make a vegetarian meal for me.

We looked shyly at each other over the white tablecloth and hearty water glasses filled with ice. I stared out the window at the line of tall cedars. The light was British Columbia gray-white, the light of my childhood. Our food came: your pile of sausages, my cabbage and sweet noodles. You asked if I liked my dinner and seemed pleased when I answered yes.

I let you lead the discussion so I could leave plenty of space for whatever you might want to say. You updated me on the shop. You asked about my mother. I gave you honest but vague answers—wanting to tell the truth, but wanting to protect her privacy. Was it my mother you wanted to talk about? You didn't follow up. We contemplated dessert.

I concluded you didn't have a message for me, but just wanted some time together. I didn't mind. The rare sweetness of being together was enough. I looked through the menu. I predicted you would order the apple pie. You ordered the apple pie. I smiled to myself. Nice some things didn't change.

Then you surprised me with a story about your mother. The winter before I was born, when you lived with my mother in a cabin on Sugarloaf Mountain above Boulder, your mother caught a flight

In Praise of Inadequate Gifts

from Philadelphia, an expensive and uncharacteristic trip.

Your mother was a proper East Coast lady: an amateur historian, a collector of dolls and antiques, a devoted member of the Episcopal church, and a member of the Lee Society for descendants of Robert E. Lee. She wore seersucker suits. She kept her house spotless; served soft-boiled eggs in egg cups; corrected pronunciation, manners, and posture, and did not discuss personal feelings: all negative emotions and bad dreams could be blamed on indigestion. You and your friends had devoted most of your energy to rebelling against her formality. So her trip, her urgency and emotion, was unlike her.

She had a story for you: When she was giving birth to you, the doctors gave her too much ether. She separated from her body, rose above her bed, and then out of the hospital. In the sky, she saw a black hole the size of the moon. On the other side of that hole was purity, beauty, light. But she'd have to die to get there. She longed for that light. But now she was a mother, so she decided not to go.

That's all you gave me. You didn't tell me how you reacted to the story—what you said back to her. That you shared the story with me felt like an offering, but I didn't know what it meant. Was it an apology for our arguments? An acknowledgement of the possibility of life after death? Or merely an unselfish gift to your mother and me— to pass along her story without insult or interpretation? Why hadn't you told me years ago, when we discussed life-after-death experiences? I knew from the past I couldn't ask any clarifying questions without muddling you, diminishing your gift. So driving home from Inglebrook, I didn't ask you what I most wanted to know: How does it feel to be close to death? How does it feel to look back over a life? In the end, what really matters?

The details from your life at that time yielded no answers. You were still legally married to your wife, but lived separately, in a relationship that was neither married nor unmarried. You'd settled in a small, half-finished industrial loft on the docks with your cat Calvin and your dog Hobbes. The walls were half-painted a mustard color with a few swipes of teal. Your plywood floor was covered in great balls of dog hair that floated around in the drafts. Your bed was

In Praise of Inadequate Gifts

in the corner, piled with a dirty plaid comforter, grimy sheets, and a child's Teenage Mutant Ninja Turtle pillowcase. Your armchair and table faced the window overlooking the docks, the bay, and your eagles, gulls, and kingfishers. Your table was stacked with bird guides and aids to help you with your daily *New York Times* crossword puzzle: an atlas, a large dictionary, a book of classical mythology, *The New York Public Library Desk Reference*, and *The New York Times Everyday Reader's Dictionary of Misunderstood, Misused, and Mispronounced Words*. I knew only that you were a man who likes water and boats and birds and puzzles and learning and time to be quiet.

Driving home from the Inglenook, I couldn't ask my questions, but my heart was welling up and I wanted to give you something—something true. And recently, I'd had a falling away of hurts, a clarity about what you had given me. My voice sounded full of water when I told you that you had given me one of my life's greatest gifts: "You gave me a love of reading and treated my questions with respect. You made me love learning."

You were silent, looking at the highway, as if you were thinking.

"I didn't try to give you that . . . It's just me."

"It's a gift anyway," I said, "one too few children have." It could hardly hold all I wanted to say, but it would have to do.

The night before your memorial, I couldn't sleep. I was stiff and restless. I tried to read an inspirational book. Then a novel. Finally, I pulled out the manila envelopes I'd gathered of your old letters to your mother you'd inherited when she died. I read and sorted them— a record of an earnest, cocky college student first touching the edges of the counterculture. Then, around two or three in the morning, I began to feel suffocated by guilt for all the years after college I hadn't seen or talked to you.

Suddenly, I felt you again.

I'm not as certain of your presence as I was of the moment in the bathroom, when your words blasted all my other thoughts, but you seemed to say, "You needed time away to find your own sense of identity. I understand."

I had three responses:

First: relief—you weren't bitter; your words were generous.

Second: frustration. That wasn't the reason I didn't talk to you; that was your reason for your estrangement from your parents.

Third: resignation. You didn't get it, but at least you weren't mad. Some things never change, and that was annoying and comforting. I slept through the rest of the night.

When my sister found out she was pregnant, she asked Prairie and you what you wanted her son to call you. Prairie chose "Granny." You answered, "Flash," I assume for Flash Gordon, your childhood hero.

Tenzin was only two and knew nothing of death when he and his dad arrived for your memorial. "Where Grandpa Flash?" he asked over and over.

My sister was too stunned and grief-stricken to decide how to explain death. For the moment, she settled on, "He's gone away." She'd figure out later what to tell him.

Not long after she'd returned home, she emailed this conversation she'd had with Tenzin in the car:

Tenzin: Mommy, I saw Flash.

Me: You did? Where?

Tenzin: In a BIG boat. He was going on a BIG trip.

Me: Did he say anything?

Tenzin: No, he's gone now.

Pause

Tenzin: He's safe for me.

Me: He's safe for you?

Tenzin: Yeah.

I wish I could debate with you now in the language of science. I'd say, "We think of ourselves as distinct and singular. But we are full of holes. The molecules that build our bodies are ninety-nine percent empty space. With the right compactor, we could squeeze ourselves down to the size of a marble. Solidity is an illusion. We picture our skin as an impermeable layer between ourselves and the outside world, but water wrinkles our fingertips. Our skin exhales nitrogen and carbon dioxide. Our body we call "one" is really an ecosystem of

In Praise of Inadequate Gifts

millions—50 million bacteria per square inch on our skin alone. We are not singular, but many, with no clear edges." I'd argue that science proves that the walls that separate us from the dead aren't as solid as we think.

On the day of your memorial, Prairie asked me to read at the service "The Cremation of Sam McGee," a silly poem you'd loved about two prospectors in the Yukon. When Sam realizes he's going to freeze to death, he makes the narrator swear to cremate him. After days of mushing, and lugging the corpse, the narrator finds an old shipwreck, throws Sam in the boiler, and lights the coal. Soon he can't resist peeking. *I guess he's cooked, and it's time I looked.* When he opens the door, Sam sits bolt upright and says, *Please close that door. It's fine in here, but I greatly fear you'll let in the cold and storm—Since I left Plumtree, down in Tennessee, it's the first time I've been warm.* Although I'm shy and grieving and know the ridiculous poem will offend some of the traditional locals, I tell Prairie I will—it's the least I could do for you whose greatest gift to me had been reading.

All day, the town members, family, and friends hustled around, buying food and cleaning up the small boat museum at the end of the dock where we would hold the memorial. I scrubbed the floors, set up tables, moved boats and old diving equipment. Then I went home and changed. When I returned, the room had been transformed. Someone had brought large bouquets of lilies. The tables were lined with hors d'oeuvres. Rima and my other sisters had assembled photographs from all eras of your life on poster boards.

The black and white portraits of you as a child and teenager shocked me. Your same far-apart eyes, but your face so smooth and gentle and bright. All fears and self-invention and accomplishments and disappointments and secrets and shame and the long decay of illness stripped away. Like Helen, your photographs were glowing. All of them. You were beautiful and radiant. I started to cry and couldn't stop until I was heaving. The reserved Canadian townspeople looked at me with pity and a little fear. I snuck out to the deck and then up some stairs to a private, hidden deck where I could fall apart in private.

A friend came to find me and whispered, "It's starting, people

In Praise of Inadequate Gifts

are asking for you." He put an arm around me and led me to the front row, to a chair reserved for me. People stared and I looked down. I looked up at the photographs and started to cry and couldn't look at you again. I cried until I stood up to read. To still myself, I pretended I was reading to my students, focused on the rhythm and silly rhyme.

There are strange things done in the midnight sun by the men who moil for gold . . .

You are gone. But now you are in the words to "The Cremation of Sam McGee." You are in my name. You are in your name. Jack. Jack Wilson. John Arnold Wilson, Junior. You are in your photographs. In your handwriting. In the names of the places you loved: Sugarloaf Mountain, Texada Island, Vancouver Island. You are in what you loved as a child: transistor radios, Pogo comics, *The Lone Ranger*, and *Sergeant Preston of the Yukon*. You are in what we all loved together when Rima and I were children: big dogs, B.C. ferries, games of Monopoly, Walt Disney's Uncle Scrooge comics, and the books you read aloud. You are in those things you never stopped loving for your whole life: ravens, gargoyles, harmonicas, the game Go, graph paper, crossword puzzles, mint chocolate chip ice cream, the *Adventures of TinTin*, the Art of M.C. Escher, *The Lord of the Rings*—especially the wizard Gandalf, who was the man you wanted to be in your old age. Maybe that-which-you-loved are beams of light—tunnels, or strings— that link us in this world to you in yours. Maybe the system is closed, but bigger than we ever imagined.

Now that you are gone, two voices joust in my mind. A childlike voice insists photos glow for me and the dead have spoken to me. I can, in rare moments—it's happened other times, too—glimpse into the veil between worlds. But an adult voice, with your reasonable tone, argues back: You're a woman in denial who will not face death, who will not look at dead bodies or the invisible ashes of mortality hanging around all our necks. You've borrowed the voices of the dead to tell yourself what you needed to hear.

I want this story to come to a neat conclusion. I want to echo the messages of the life-after-death books, that the purpose of life is to love and learn. I want to conclude that, although I can't be sure where you've gone, I can find you in that which you have loved. That's the lesson for us all: love well, love broadly, leave little bits of ourselves behind—tucked into whatever it is we have loved.

But there is something else.

I thought I'd made progress in letting go of my hungry curiosity about you—and I have—but here I am again, making the same mistake I did when you were alive, badgering you in my search for messages and meaning.

Now, Jack Arnold Wilson, it is time for me to set aside questing for what I will never find, asking for what is not mine to know, hoping for what you cannot give, and trying to make your story mine. You have told me exactly what you want me to know. *"I'm okay."*

It's time for me to leave you in peace.

A NARRATIVE BREAK:
ON READING AFTER CRISIS

In three years' time, my life as I knew it cracked. My father, in his early sixties, passed on. A year later, my mother died suddenly, age fifty-nine, of an undiagnosed illness. The following year, a surprise to both my husband and me, our long marriage disintegrated. Grief piled upon grief, and in their wake, I lost all desire to read. I had been a voracious reader all my life and, in the months following these losses, its absence unhinged me, even more than the recent loss of my house, possessions, and familiar routines.

Slowly, slowly, over two years, I found my way back to books, but through the most unlikely of avenues. And in some ways my reading rituals have been—perhaps permanently—altered. But why did crisis so radically change my reading habits?

To understand how deeply the loss of reading disoriented me, you have to know my reading history. As a child, each time we moved again, I unpacked my books first, organized them by category, and arranged them in size order on my bookshelves. I adored the books of E.B. White: *Charlotte's Web. The Trumpet of the Swan.* I read and reread the Wizard of Oz books and the complete Laura Ingalls Wilder Little House series. I melted into the worlds of Roald Dahl in *Charlie and the Chocolate Factory, Charlie and the Great Glass Elevator,* and *James and the Giant Peach,* and yellow Nancy Drew books overflowed two of my shelves. Books filled in the gaps of my interrupted education—and were friends who could move with me. I was shy, but books gave me intimacy: companions who understood me and a window into the hearts of those different from me. Stories were an escape. Almost always, we lived in cramped, noisy apartments and books provided quiet, private worlds that belonged only to me.

Stories also gave me a way to manage my feelings. My mother's emotions were enormous and unpredictable. She'd yell at her boss, quit her job, and again we'd move and suffer months without an income, sometimes days without food. For me, emotions had life-threatening consequences, so I vowed to keep mine as even as possible. But within the structured confines of book covers, guided by a wise author-consciousness I trusted to keep me safe, I could feel the full range of anger, fear, and grief. I could risk hope.

My parents, as part of the sixties rebellion against the staid formality of the fifties, were exploring new moral codes, so their value systems were murky and changing. The books I read were not didactic, but the authors held hard-earned philosophies for living well, which imbued their stories. Unbeknownst to me, and under my atheist father's radar, I was absorbing books by Christian authors: C.S. Lewis's *The Lion, the Witch, and the Wardrobe* and his Chronicles of Narnia, Madeleine L'Engle's *A Wrinkle in Time, A Wind in the Door,* and a *Swiftly Tilting Planet.* They gifted me with a moral center. Most importantly, books gave me models to live by: story after story in which unlikely children became heroes, masters of their own destiny, of service to others. They were flawed, but brave and unselfish. They endured. They thrived. I didn't realize it at the time, but I was building a story frame on which I could model my life: a map through my childhood to a meaningful adulthood. Books were full of drama—but not senseless drama. Suffering was necessary for the characters' growth, to test their mettle, refine their characters, and arrive at a happy end. I, too, was on a hero's journey, and I would prevail.

Although we had little money while I was growing up, my mother indulged my book habit. When I was in early elementary school, she hand-rolled her cigarettes, and every time we visited the tobacco/book shop, she let me buy a new novel. In seventh grade, I was immersed in *Watership Down* and reading it during history class. The boy in front of me hid my book and wouldn't give it back. That night, my mother, who understood how dreadful it was to be interrupted in the middle of a story, drove me on icy Colorado roads to buy another copy. The next day I was again reading *Watership Down* at my desk, and the boy, bewildered, pulled out the book hidden behind the magazines lining the tray of the blackboard. "I was going to give it to you today . . . You must really like reading."

By the time I was an adult, my reading had probably evolved from a healthy habit into something closer to a compulsion. Years ago, I read *The Artist's Way*, a twelve-week creativity program, which

In Praise of Inadequate Gifts

asks participants to sacrifice reading for a week. I exhibited all the behaviors of an addict. Excuses. Justifications. As an English teacher, I *had* to prepare the reading for class and grade my papers, right? And I'm such a quick reader, I *involuntarily* read the sides of buses and backs of cereal boxes. And, really, who can help at least opening a *People* magazine at the hairdresser? Okay, maybe when I found myself in the bathtub reading the ingredient list on the shampoo bottles, I recognized I had a problem.

Addicts have reasons for their behavior—for me, reading was a way to settle my busy mind. Here were my dominant obsessions: reviewing my to-do list; monitoring my fussy emotions; critiquing my flawed body parts; fearing I'm in dire danger of disappointing someone; mulling over my relationships; envisioning my future and evaluating my progress toward it; worrying over the news; grieving about environmental issues; managing memories of the past; second-guessing myself, and mostly berating myself for not living up to impossibly high standards. Reading anything was a form of rest. Reading narrowed my thoughts to what was on the page and its thin band of related associations. It gave my thought some structure, an escape from the crazier parts of myself.

So how could such a compulsive reader lose such a deeply ingrained habit? Yes, the stresses of those few years were unusual: in addition to the deaths of both parents, divorce, and my challenging job as a high school teacher, I was enrolled in a rigorous master's degree program. My father-in-law, who'd been an artistic mentor to me, unexpectedly died the same weekend as my mother. Just after my husband and I separated, I fell in love—this was joyful, but also overwhelming and disorienting. But none of these were more than the ordinary changes of an ordinary human life. Less shocking than some of the insanity of my childhood. So why had this confluence of events stalled, for the first time, my reading?

Later, I spent hours researching how stress affects reading and found nothing more revealing than this common-sense statement on a website on grief: loss affects focus and concentration, and "You may read a paragraph several times and still not absorb its meaning." Grief disrupts concentration and the ability to track a story. But why? What was happening in my brain? I don't know, but I have a partial theory: loss is traumatic to the degree to which it disrupts a sense of identity. In my childhood, my story of myself had not yet solidified, and I was partially aware, even then, that my crises were largely of my parents' making. I didn't take the disruptions personally.

But as an adult, without realizing it, I'd grown into a story of myself, particularly in my marriage. I'd promised myself I would not repeat the multiple divorces of my parents. I believed my "I do" was a commitment for life. I was yoked to my marriage by my spiritual beliefs, the hopes of friends and family, the intermingling of finances and possessions, and, finally, after years, a surrender to the loneliness at the center of our relationship. So the sudden dissolution of my marriage, complicated soon after by the new man in my life, was a shock and a wound and a confusion—an unraveling of my story of myself. I was not the character I thought I was. The plot was not moving toward its expected end. There was nothing left to resolve but to love my parents and my spouse and let them go. But who was I in this new and open space?

So that's my theory: change is traumatic to the degree it explodes our story. Recovery depends on our ability to let that story wash away—and our willingness to examine the life left behind and, to the best of our ability, see it as it really is.

That explanation, in itself, is a story, so I can't be sure of it. I'm certain of so little these days. But here's what I do know: In the months after the deaths and the separation, my thoughts stalled. My busy mind had been shocked into silence. I had to keep going: teach my classes, grade my papers, do my homework, answer my work emails. But it took almost more energy than I had. Several days after my mother's death, a friend invited me to a small gathering at her house. "Come, it will be good for you to see people," she said. She couldn't know how stunned I was, how a loss can be like an injury, how I needed to keep still, how I couldn't make small talk—or worse, meaningful talk.

At that point reading felt like small talk and meaningful talk in the living room of my brain. Too exhausting. I could no longer argue politics with news magazines or fret over the unfolding facts with newspapers. I couldn't have emotional conversations with novels

In Praise of Inadequate Gifts

about desire and suffering. Short stories demanded focus I didn't have. Self-help books were full of lectures and advice I couldn't follow. In the past, fine literature—the best thinking by the best minds— restored me, but even these fine authors' words were too much of someone else rattling around in my head. I needed to be alone.

Here is the moment I knew my mother was going to die: My sister and I had moved her to a care facility. She loved birds and was fond of the sweet stuffed animals my sister and I sent her over the years. To make her room cozier, I brought her some items from her house: A little teddy bear. Some small paper-mache birds with real feathers she'd bought to decorate packages. While she was sleeping, I set them around the room. When she awoke, she almost panicked: "Take them away! I need you to take them away." I gathered them and, tears welling, had to leave the room.

As soon as I was gone, my mother told my sister she feared she had hurt my feelings. But that wasn't it. Even though she had not been given a diagnosis, for some reason I can't explain, I knew her need to have her room stripped bare meant she was going to die soon. In retrospect, I believe all her attention was focused on her struggle; she was both fighting for her life and preparing to set down the ultimate book, the story that was her own human existence. She couldn't bear any clutter or distraction.

As I adjusted to life without my mother, my mind craved the same extreme simplicity; reading felt like clutter.

In the months after my losses, my relationship to time altered. I could see only the present moment or the cosmic scale. I had lost my capacity for long-term planning and could think no farther ahead than the next day's lesson plans. On the positive side, I was emotionally present with my students in a way I'd never been. In the past I'd been most emotionally alive while reading; now I was inhabiting my own life, strange and disorienting though it was.

On the other hand, I suddenly saw human life on the largest scale, the great wide arc of human history. My attention shifted from my goals for the week, my five-year plan, even my own lifespan, to eons passing: thousands of generations, born and dying, born and dying. What is meaningful in this vast measure? I couldn't care less

In Praise of Inadequate Gifts

about the small dramas of Hollywood stars that had secretly attracted me: who was dating whom and who had adopted a baby and who had lost too much weight. They will get old and die. They had their own griefs, just like mine, and I wanted to give them some privacy. Likewise, on public radio, I'd hear pundits, with great intensity and earnestness, micro-analyzing the possible outcomes of an election over which they had no influence or control. "You'll know soon enough," I thought to myself, wearied by the urgency in their voices. "And what does it matter anyway? We all die." The enormous boulder of time, with its births and deaths and revolutions, would continue to roll, with or without their words.

This was also new for me: I was grieving in real time. In the past, I'd coped with crises through elaborate mechanisms of denial: immediate numbness, followed much later by confusing emotions that leaked out at unexpected, and sometimes inappropriate, moments. This time was different. I cried often. Small pleasures—the taste of an orange, the warm water of a bath, the beauty of a bouquet sent by a friend—were magnified. All emotions were heightened—as if I had no exterior skin to dull suffering or joy. The longing in a song on the radio, the tender loneliness in a painting, the vulnerable expression on a student's face: I felt them all with overwhelming intensity.

In the months after the initial shock of the losses had lessened, instead of reading, I wanted to see people. I said yes to more invitations. I didn't want to talk about myself, but I wanted to hear others tell their stories. Over and over, I guided every conversation to the same essential question: "What's the worst thing that ever happened to you and how did you get through it?" And people talked, strangers and acquaintances and friends who had never before told their secrets. Their stories floated in the air rather than sitting on a page. I didn't know if I would ever return to reading—or who I would be without it. I fretted about this but had to let my worry go, as no amount of effort could restore my former reading habits.

And then, slowly my books did return to me—but not in the way I had imagined.

My sister, also going through a divorce, mailed me the *Tao Te Ching*, the sixth century Chinese Taoist text, translated into English

In Praise of Inadequate Gifts

and arranged in poetic lines by Stephen Mitchell. It was the first, and for a while, only book I could read. To understand how unusual this was, you have to know my pre-crisis reading habits. During the summer, I'd gobble whatever I could get my hands on, often with some inexplicable theme: novels and memoirs about the Holocaust, memoirs by outdoorswomen of the 1940s, everything by and about Anne Morrow Lindberg. But once the school year began, the books on my bedside table turned predictable: 1. A half-finished literary novel, which, as soon as my job got too demanding, I abandoned. (But if anyone asked me what I was reading, I'd mention it.) 2. A memoir, which I was reading steadily or couldn't put down. 3. A self-help book I'd read a little of every day, but which I might tuck in a drawer when my literary friends came over. 4. A book about writing or spirituality that I usually read in the morning. 5. A book of essays. I'd read a few pages before bed every night. 6. A layman's book of sociology or psychology that I'd read in fragments. 7. A book of poetry I'd intended to read but never opened.

I predicted that when I started reading again, I'd begin with gentle, amusing books, which had soothed me when I was most overwhelmed by work—say, the travel writing of Bill Bryson. Or maybe a spiritual memoir on death or divorce, which would simultaneously name my feelings and give me a comforting spiritual context for them. But, no. I found my way back to reading by reading what I had long avoided: poetry. And not just any poetry, but the most abstract and impersonal of poetry.

As a child, I loved poetry, the singsong voices and rhythms, the nonsense and surprise. In college, when I began taking traditional literature classes, I became enamored of poetry again. I remember buying T.S. Eliot's *The Four Quartets* and reading it alone in my dorm room on a Friday night. The rhythms and language ("We shall not cease from exploration/And the end of all our exploring/Will be to arrive where we started/And know the place for the first time") felt so intense and beautiful and true and transcendent that my body filled with tingles. I didn't know what to do with those tingles, couldn't contain them, so I did what any serious student of poetry might do in the same situation: I jumped on the bed and yelled a quiet-girl yell.

After college I called myself a poetry-lover but I did not become a poetry reader. There were three obstacles. One: The tingles. The sensation was pleasurable but so intense I feared being overwhelmed. Two: After college, I slipped into the ordinary life of trying to find a job and learning to be an adult, navigating new and old relationships, and, living on my own for the first time, processing my tumultuous childhood. Poetry reminded me that I was no longer living with a child's sense of awe and wonder, which made me feel dull. Three: My busy mind worried and raced. Reading poetry required a shift of consciousness, a stillness I could rarely muster. Year after year, I bought new poetry books. I kept them near me but didn't open them.

Why, then, did my reading recovery begin with the *Tao Te Ching*, especially poetry so spare and abstract? "Free from desire, you realize only the mystery. Caught in desire, you see only the manifestations." Perhaps it was the unexpected hibernation of my busy brain. I had lost my ability for long-term planning, but taking its place was a quietness in which I could receive poetry. And the Tao was so pared to its essence as to have almost no sense of a human author. My mind did not feel invaded by a guest whose personality I had to accommodate; the words felt as if the universe itself was speaking. "Can you deal with the most vital matters by letting events take their course?" "Can you love people and love them without imposing your will?" It encouraged release even from my goals and striving: "When her work is done, she forgets it. That is why it lasts forever." Most of all, it promised that even though my story had dissolved and I had no framework with which to understand myself, I still existed. I copied this line many times in my journal: "Because she has let go of herself, she is perfectly fulfilled."

I read the slim volume over and over, and then moved on to the complete poems of Rumi, the thirteenth century Persian mystic. Rumi's writing has a more distinct personality, an identity with which I could agree or argue but, similarly, his words promised that right in the midst of my jumble-thoughts was wisdom: "Where did I come from and what am I supposed to be doing? I have no idea." Rumi helped me accept my blasted state—"This year I am a burnt kabob"—and embrace a larger definition of myself: "Drink all your passion and be a disgrace." He comforted me: "Be empty of worrying. Think who created thought." He promised me a future beyond my suffering: "Look at the chefs preparing special plates for everyone, according to what they need." "Why do you stay in the prison when the door is so wide open? Walk out like someone suddenly born into color. Do it now." At that time, only poetry could reach through my fog of grief and fear.

Not long after my father died, I took an afternoon workshop with the cross-genre writer Greg Glazner on the difference between narrative and lyric writing. Narrative, or traditional storytelling, he explained, unfolds in time. It takes place in a specific location and moves from here to there (through change in plot, place, or thought) along a timeline. In experimental work, the line may be fragmented, the location surreal or subjective, but the work is still grounded by time. Lyrical writing, on the other hand, transcends time. It stretches above the flow of story to touch some timeless illumination. It glimpses a dimension where contradictions are reconciled, stretches toward insight for which mere words are inadequate. The *Tao* and Rumi.

I had experienced both birth and death as lyric moments, existing outside the familiar flow of time. When I visit friends just after the birth of their baby, I always feel as if I'm entering another dimension. An atmosphere profoundly still, yet alive. Hushed, reverent, alert. In those first few weeks, the room where the family rests feels filled with a warm, protective layer, where time moves slowly, if at all. I have felt the same timeless, reverent hush just after a death. For a moment, everyone's stories, fears, hungers are stilled. Worrying stalls. I know suddenly (and can't imagine I will ever forget again, but I always do) that life is for living and loving and nothing else matters. The ache of loss has not yet permeated: I feel in the presence of mystery.

None of us knows, really, from whence we come and where we go when we slip to and from this world of human time—this elaborate story we have told ourselves about ourselves. At moments of birth or death, we are jarred from our story, touch the lyric, transcendent level. So maybe that is what happened to me: The narrative of my life had been broken. My parents had disappeared through a crack into another dimension. My marriage, which had given shape to my life and grounded me in space and time and relationship, evaporated. In the months afterward, I was forced to return to my story, my life unfolding in time, but I did so on autopilot. My mind still dwelled in the timeless, placeless, formless lyrical. Only poetry made sense.

In the years since, I have settled again into the shape of an ordinary life. I plan for my classes, and my future, and worry again about my to-do list. I can't resist the headlines of the celebrity magazines in the grocery store. The familiar stack and range of reading material sits heaped beside my bed.

But all is not as it was. Although I'm no longer the world-weary person who sighs over the great arc of human history, I feel more distant from political debates. My energy level is slower but more intense. Now, I can slow myself down enough to read poetry. I find it easier to hold contradictory truths: I read Christian philosophers and Zen monks without a sense I'm betraying either one. At first, I couldn't find my way back to novels—my first love—on my own, so I joined a book group to help get me there.

And my reading process has altered. I read more slowly. And I re-read. Sentences. Passages. Whole books—I revisit old loves, or begin a book again as soon as I have finished. I feel anguish sometimes about all the reading I'll miss in my lifetime, but I can't make myself read any faster. I use my intuition to choose my books and abandon those that don't speak to me. All this is new. I don't know if the changes in my reading habits are permanent, but I suspect I will never be the same reader I had been.

One ritual has stayed blessedly the same. I'm decades from my childhood, but when I moved with my new beau into our new house, I was most eager to open my book boxes. I held my old and soon-to-be-read companions in my hand. I felt their weight. I sorted them into categories, arranged them by size, and set them on my shelves.

They surround me now. They are the ballasts that keep me steady and close to the earth and secret doors through which I slip into another universe; they are weighted and light, grounding and expansive. They are my history. They are my future. They exist outside of time. They are friendly and patient as they wait for me. They vibrate a little, as if alive.

In Praise of Inadequate Gifts

BIG KITTY

A few years before the end of my marriage, while cross-country skiing in Tahoe, I saw my first cougar tracks, enormous, in the snow.

"Mountain lion!" I yelled to my husband, who slid up behind me.

My whole body felt balloon light. A tremble moved through me. I sped after the tracks into an aspen grove. The mountain lion I'd been seeking for years was near.

My husband, who rarely raised his voice, screamed after me: "Stop!"

I paused, reluctantly.

He was a cautious man. Although we were only on a quick afternoon ski through a field, rarely out of sight of the highway where we had parked our car, he insisted we both carry full safety bags with flashlights, extra batteries, matches, rope, space blankets, chemical hand warmers, and compasses. Other skiers whizzed through the meadow in their tights and light jackets. We trudged with our backpacks, extra layers, water, and food to last us days.

I couldn't argue with his rules, since snowstorms can come up at any time. On days I felt patient with his protocols, I'd goodheartedly tease him, calling him "Safety Man!" He'd laugh, raise his index finger and say, "Safety first!"

But over the years, what had been a natural caution supported by worst-case scenarios had morphed into something closer to paranoia. He was afraid to let me drive more than a twenty-mile radius from our house, so each longer trip involved a fight. I couldn't park my car on the street because it might be hit. And the rules for inside the house were getting more and more complex. The system I must use to wash the dishes. The system I must use to clean the rabbit's cage. He was fearful of identity theft and didn't trust my recycling abilities, so before the paper went out, he sorted through every piece again to make sure I hadn't left any identifying marks on any scrap. He adjusted my flame when I boiled water.

In my effort to sooth his anxieties, I shaped myself around

In Praise of Inadequate Gifts

them. But instead of feeling eased by his rituals, my husband's rigidities grew. The TV shows we could watch, our sources for news, the music he could bear, the circle of people he could trust—all shrunk. The unhappier he became with our house, his job, our community, the more stubborn his fear of change. And the more I felt trapped by love and obligation in our withering life.

But now my mountain lion was here, and my husband's "Stop!" felt like all his other narrow prohibitions. All I had to do was follow those big cat feet.

I skied a few more yards.

"No!" he screamed. Real panic filled his voice, not the grouchy tone of our usual power tugs. That surprised me. I stopped.

"Why?"

He sounded close to tears. "You could be killed, that's why!"

Well, there was always that. I had just proved to him again I was profoundly lacking in common sense and he must, from now on, keep a keener eye on me.

I knew my husband was right: I probably shouldn't speed after a hunting wildcat with nothing to protect me but ski poles and a childish wish that the cougar might be happy to see me. I turned back.

What had impelled me to take such a risk?

My love of mountain lions, also called cougars, began in elementary school—that time when choosing your favorite animal is serious business, as important as choosing your Halloween costume. Your favorite animal is your alter ego, the window to your soul. You may look like that gangly girl last picked for kickball, but if your favorite animal is a wildcat, the other children might glimpse the strength and beauty trapped inside.

In the beginning of fourth grade, my favorite animal was the tiger. Tiger starts with a T, like my name. That seemed important. On the outside, I was shy, tall, freakishly skinny, with twisted teeth that gapped in front and short hair that stood up in every direction, but inside I was a tiger, graceful and mysterious. Part of me, though, was uneasy with my choice. Tigers seemed too bright—that black on orange, with glassy yellow eyes. Too jazzy.

Later that year, through my elementary school Scholastic

In Praise of Inadequate Gifts

Book Club, I ordered a book about North American wildcats, stuffed with photos and facts about lynx, bobcats, and mountain lions. As soon as I reached the images of the yellow cats, I felt instant recognition. I, too, had dry blond hair. The mountain lion ranges the length of the western U.S. into Canada, and—since I lived in Colorado and visited my father in British Columbia—that was my range, too. A mountain lion was a tiger without the jazz. I was a mountain lion.

But maybe there was more to my choice than I could see at the time. As a child, I tried desperately to be good. Since my mother suffered regular mental breakdowns, which kept our lives in constant chaos, I tried to be the stable center: neat, dependable, predictable, and self-controlled. In contrast, the cats (to borrow from a Mary Oliver poem) seemed *wild, amoral, reckless, peaceful.* Perhaps I wanted to be a mountain lion because part of me wanted to escape my self-imposed confines.

Or maybe they represented a strength I needed. Chris Bolgiano, who wrote *Mountain Lion: An Unnatural History of Pumas and People,* loves the way mountain lions seem both male and female: "Then there is the matter of their sleekness and agility, the quintessence of feline grace, and their shy mystery. These qualities are deeply feminine, but mountain lions couple them with sinewy strength that is savagely masculine." Maybe there's something to that. Timid, raised with a sister by a single mother, who was raised by a single mother, who was raised by a single mother, maybe I craved some gender wholeness. I wanted power and control, without giving up grace.

Perhaps I saw mountain lions as overgrown house cats—my trusted friends from my childhood, but big enough to embrace me. When I was in high school, my mother told me this mountain lion story (she'd heard it from her sister in Loveland, Colorado, who had, in turn, heard it from a park ranger):

A couple with a toddler went camping in the Colorado mountains. Early evening, the little girl wandered from the campsite, wearing only a dress and a light nylon jacket. When her parents couldn't find her, a growing team of rescuers staged an all-night

In Praise of Inadequate Gifts

search. Temperatures plummeted to hypothermia-inducing cold.

The next morning, they found the girl curled in a ball in the middle of the trail. When her father scooped her into his arms, she was toasty-warm. She blinked awake.

"You're so warm!" he said.

She nestled into his chest. "I slept with the big kitty."

A mountain lion. A mountain lion had wrapped itself around her to keep her warm through the night. The story made me cry.

I've researched the story and found no proof of its veracity. But I want the big kitty story to be true. Maybe what I really want is to be that girl—to have all that tawny softness wrapped around me. A purr. A deep, primitive mother love.

When I first moved to the San Francisco Bay Area, married and in my mid-twenties, the golden hills looked to me like enormous sleeping mountain lions, yellow fur rippling over their muscles, the tight folds and bends. When I learned those golden hills hosted golden cats, I tried, for years, to find one.

At dawn and dusk, when mountain lions are most active, I jogged remote trails, hoping for a glimpse. The cats are difficult to track: the trails are hard-packed, so when the weather's dry, wild animal prints are light and dusty; when it rains, they are clay-slippery and smeared, mingled with marks from hiking boots, horse shoes, running shoes, mountain bikes, large dogs, and kids who drag their feet. Besides, the cats tend to avoid the trail. They slink through the leafy forest floor and huddle in the chaparral.

But they were there. Every week, the local news listed sightings. This drove me wild with frustration. Because I really looked. On a long hike or run, I watched the way the ecosystem changed: riparian, redwood, live oaks and bays, chaparral. I found hidden springs. I identified ferns, flowers, and mosses. I knew the animal signs: squirrel stashes, woodpecker holes, coyote scat, the rototilled earth where the wild boars had been nosing around for snacks. I knew eucalyptus and bay trees by smell alone. But I couldn't see a house cat magnified ten times. How could I miss something so beautiful and enormous?

During my years of searching, my image of a cougar as a safe, warm kitty has been complicated. A year before I found my mountain lion tracks in the snow, my husband and I were hiking in a local preserve and spotted a mysterious hose in the underbrush. We followed it, bushwhacking up the steep chaparral-sided mountain, just a few miles from the heart of Silicon Valley, until we stumbled upon an elaborate marijuana operation: hundreds of plants cleverly camouflaged in the shade of the coyote brush to avoid helicopter detection. My husband said he'd heard stories, that the drug lords from Mexico donated their Uzi-carrying guards to protect their crop, so when we saw the camera rigged in the crook of a tree, we hightailed it, crawling on our hands and knees under the scratchy brush, heading for what we hoped was a trail. And that's where we saw it. The deer. Dragged under the bushes, its ribcage ripped open, all internal organs missing.

I've learned the cats make no warning sound, attack from behind, and can leap twelve feet in the air and spring twenty-five feet forward from a standstill. Almost every local public trailhead hosts a sign with instructions and diagrams on how to prevent a mountain lion attack: Move in groups. Pick up your small children. Try to appear larger than you are. Wave your arms. Make loud noises. And don't run: you might appear to be prey. I've read the articles, like the one about a woman in Southern California, running alone, shredded by a cougar.

So I have become more afraid. Sometimes I've run trails at sunset, not with the intent of finding a mountain lion, but just playing outside before the day ends. I'm heading toward the ridge, the sage and coyote brush turning rose-gold in the setting sun, and I'm suddenly overcome by terror that a mountain lion is near. At the bend, my imaginary lion crouches and I'm washed with panic and sprint, running from the very cat I've been hunting all these years.

Other times, alone on remote stretches of trail, usually on a bend not far from a creek, I've felt something. A presence. Someone watching me. Perhaps the senses-under-my-senses perceived a great warmth crouched behind a boulder or a fallen tree, camouflaged by dried yellow leaves; heard the low heartbeat, the quiet breathing; smelled something earthy, musky. In these times, I was neither afraid nor not afraid. Just very awake. Pure animal.

About halfway through my marriage, I signed up for a short, silent retreat at a monastery. The quiet was punctuated by sessions in which we were given writing prompts and opportunities to share. In the hours of uninterrupted reflection, as I wrote in my journal in the dappled shade of the sugar maples, I stumbled upon a truth:

Although I tried to make room for play in my life, the anxious, hardworking child had grown into an anxious, hardworking adult. I ruled myself with rigid expectations about how I could use my time, high standards for productivity, and an overburdened sense of responsibility to others. I'd not yet admitted to myself my marriage was dying, nor how stifling it had become. I wrote in large letters a sentence I didn't fully understand, but which felt true: *I have anorexia of the soul.*

Several years later, mountain lions started wandering the city streets of Palo Alto where I teach, slinking along streambeds that run behind houses, padding along sidewalks at dawn. One of my high school students, a girl from Russia whose hobbies were clothes shopping and hip-hop music, mentioned casually at the start of my class, "Yeah, so this morning, on the way to school, I saw this mountain lion outside my apartment building." I wanted to jump up and down and stamp my feet. How had she, who hadn't been searching, who hardly cared, found the cat I'd been hunting for years?

The lions worried the residents, and when one was found lurking near an elementary school, officials shot it. They dissected the body for clues to its unusual boldness. Young, a male—and starving. Biologists guessed a bumper crop of kittens had just reached adulthood, the time when the males leave their mothers to establish their own territories. Their ranges are large, and with the older males already established, the boys had nowhere to go but to where food, shelter, and safety were scarce.

Apparently, I'm not the only one obsessed with mountain lions. According to the *Guinness Book of World Records*, the mountain lion has more names than any other mammal. I knew four: *mountain lion, cougar, panther, puma.* The longer list, what I could find, reads like a poem. A chant. *Catamount, deer cat, fire cat, ghost cat, king cat, painted cat, shadow cat, silver cat, sneak cat, mountain cat, mountain demon,*

In Praise of Inadequate Gifts

mountain devil, mountain screamer. Screamer. American lion, Mexican lion, silver lion, brown tiger, red tiger. Purple feather. Indian devil. Ghost walker. To the Chickasaws, the mountain lion is *Koe-Ishto*, the *"Cat of God."*

Biologists guess the mountain lion has so many names because of its wide range. I think it's more. Although they are large animals and pace to the very edges of civilization, they are elusive. Silent, secretive, nearly invisible. We know basic facts about mountain lions, their calls and hunting habits, but their essence is a mystery. So we can project onto them the best and worst of our own interior animal being. King. Devil.

I try to resist turning the mountain lion into a metaphor. I believe animals should be solely themselves, not symbols. Yet, for years, mountain lions have sneaked into my dreams: One grips my forearm and drags me to the ocean's edge, wrestling me into the waves. It wants to drown me. I writhe and pull, but I'm losing the fight, swallowing water. Then I remember that to tame a mountain lion, I have to tickle its chin. With my free hand I rub the sweet fur under its mouth. Slowly, the shadow cat relaxes its jaw. The lion yields to my affection and releases me.

Or, I'm driving through a wild-animal park. A mountain lion pounces on the roof with a thud. We stop. The cat sinks its head down over the windshield. We're happy to see each other. It presses its mouth against the glass; I press my mouth against the glass. We give each other a kiss. I laugh.

These dreams beg for interpretation. But, upon waking, I didn't analyze them. The mountain lions seemed so real, so alive, so like friends, it didn't occur to me to turn them into symbols.

Recently, I re-read the journal I kept during my unhappy first year of marriage. I found this obscure entry, a single line with no context:

I dreamed I read God's words, 'Thy paws are unshackled.'

I won't share much of the small, private story of my marriage's end. But I can say that my husband was angry, he left, he didn't know when he'd be back. In his absence, something shifted. Space. Sunlight shining through the window. Stillness. Breath. Suddenly I could see what I hadn't let myself see before—how small I'd let myself become. And when, soon, he wanted desperately to return, I could not let him. Always before—bound by my promises, my spiritual beliefs, my certainty I could save our relationship if I only worked harder, if I changed myself—I'd tried again. But this time, finally, no matter how fervently I tried to convince myself, I could not.

Not long after the end of my marriage, I started dating a friend, a man sixteen years my junior. I had recently turned forty. Women over forty who date younger men are sometimes called cougars. Had I finally become the cat I had sought? Valerie Gibson, former sex and relationship columnist of the *Toronto Times* and guru of cougar-ness defines a cougar: "She's confident, stylish, sophisticated and sexy, and she knows exactly what she wants (hot young men and lots of great sex)." Most definitions of cougar on the site Urban Dictionary use the hunting metaphor: "On the hunt for a younger man . . . waiting, watching, calculating; gearing up to sink her claws into an innocent young and strapping buck who happens to cross her path."

I hadn't been hunting for a younger man. I hadn't been hunting for a man. Mine was a surprise and a gift. He was light-hearted and generous. Affectionate and steady. Funny. A good listener. The qualities for which I was most hungry, the essential and missing nutrients. And we had this in common: an enormous amount of stored up love and no place to put it. A kind of loneliness, but not a greedy kind—a kind that wants to give what we have to someone who wants it. I was not a high-heeled power cat of the websites. I was the starving mountain lion in the Palo Alto streambed.

I try to let the mountain lion be fully and only her elusive and mysterious animal self. Yet she's the shape of my California golden hills. She pads into my dreams and I chase her footprints in the snow. She is longing and fear. I search for her and I'm terrified of her. I don't think I *am* a cougar, but I *have* a cougar—a great golden secret—slinking inside me, moving in ways I don't understand. I can't see her or hear her, but she leaves footprints across my snowy interior.

On the difficult days after separating from my husband, when

I was overcome with guilt about leaving my old life, I feared my interior cougar was a devil bent on the destruction of my family, who had pounced on my jugular vein and eaten my interior organs. Other days I believed she wasn't evil, but amoral: driven purely by instinct, by hunger. And she'd been starving to death. This is what I hope: she's the god *Koe-Ishto,* agent of the Great Creator, who nosed me past my narrow social conventions, nudged me toward happiness. In the cat bible of my dreams, she roars, "Thy paws are unshackled!" She jumps on my car and kisses me on the mouth. I tickle her chin. She's my Big Kitty. She's wrapped herself around me in my dark night. She saved my life.

OLD LAUNDROMATS

I don't want to be here, in an un-air-conditioned laundromat on a Sunday afternoon while temperatures hover over a hundred in a strange September Silicon Valley heat wave, but I need clean clothes. My washer is broken and won't be fixed for weeks.

I drag my baskets through the smudged glass doors and am transported to the laundromats of my childhood. The rusty, lumbering washers. A few handwritten out-of-order signs. Mismatched Formica countertops for folding. The dusty floor. The metal carts for hauling wet clothes to the dryer and dry clothes to the folding tables—the same ones in which my sister and I wildly wheeled each other. The rattle-clunk of the washers rocking as they spin. The whir of the enormous dryers, the heavy flump of the clothes inside, the rhythmic click of buttons and snaps against the metal drums.

I'd been grouchy, tossing my clothes in the car, but now, as I load my machines, I'm surprised by a wash of relief, a release of breath I didn't know I was holding, a feeling edging toward joy.

In my early elementary years, my mother owned neither a car nor a washer and dryer, so she—my sister and I in tow—lugged the laundry to the laundromat on the bus in black plastic garbage bags. We always waited too long—until the annoyance of rinsing underwear in the sink and pulling on stiff and fruity jeans outweighed the grief of a lost weekend day—and we finally swung the loaded garbage bags over our shoulders. The cheap bags stretched down our backs as we walked. I used all my strength to keep mine from dragging along the sidewalk, tearing holes.

But this childhood memory doesn't explain why the tension releases from my face and shoulders as I sit cross-legged on a folding table, waiting for the washers to finish.

During those childhood days in the laundromat, time stretched into hot, vibrating dullness. My sister and I wore ourselves out with hyper cart pushing. We crawled into the empty dryers—caves just our size—to press our hands against the hole-punched metal

In Praise of Inadequate Gifts

barrels. Our mother, afraid we'd get locked inside, hauled us out. Then we all bickered. I pressed my face into the bundle of dry clothes to breathe in the clean warmth, but the piles were mountainous. So many socks without partners. Shirts already wrinkling. Sheets too big to fold alone, too big even for two children, so my sister and I fought, then angrily wadded them. The hot commercial dryers sucked the color right out of the clothes, making our favorites look thrift-store faded.

Maybe this is what pleases me about my neighborhood laundromat, even in the heavy heat: the sheer physicality of it. In this land of iPads and iPhones, most other machines take a gentle touch: The lightest swish of your finger and the world parts. Or no touch at all: Wave your phone in front of a scanner to pay for coffee and numbers pass through the air, technology so advanced it might be magic. But his laundromat requires you to gather quarters—an old-fashioned job in itself—and press them into metal slots, calling back my toddler days when there was nothing more satisfying than pushing an object into its properly shaped hole. Star-in-the-star, square-in-the-square. Oh, the triangle won't fit there. But, ah, it fits here.

My quarters keep being rejected and clattering into the coin return slot, so I experiment. I push a quarter in hard and fast, then hear the satisfying clink-clunk into some invisible bucket. Ah. Then I get to press an old-fashioned, stubborn black button to choose the temperature. The machine releases its noisy rush of water.

The last time I was in a laundromat was five years ago. It was hot then, too, in the nineties, another unexpected autumn heat wave. I'd flown to see my mother in Colorado because, she told me over the phone, she'd been ill. She could use a little help. She hadn't told me, or admitted to herself, how sick she was. My sister met me in Denver, and while she took care of phone calls to get our mother more assistance, I volunteered for the laundromat. My sister felt guilty abandoning me with so many garbage bags, but in the midst of my shock at my mother's state, I was happy for a specific job, something to do with my hands. Happy to be alone but not alone. Strangers attended to their laundry as machines shook and thumped—my

In Praise of Inadequate Gifts

personal rhythm section. I sat cross-legged on a folding table and watched a dryer window: someone had thrown in a few colorful T-shirts with their billowing white sheets. Round and round, colors flashed by, soothing as tropical fish circling a tank.

I folded ten loads. My mother, who had few other possessions, owned many clothes, most from trips to Goodwill to create a pretty wardrobe on a small budget. I pressed my face into her warm sheets. I stacked her clothes—now all too big for her—in piles: pants, skirts, short-sleeved shirts, long-sleeved shirts. Another childhood pleasure, like sorting Halloween candy or separating plastic farm animals from the African ones. I packed everything back into the garbage bags.

A week later, my mother would die and I would donate the clothes back to Goodwill in those same bags. But that night, on what would be her last night at home, I gave her what I could: a fresh nightgown and clean sheets on her bed.

Although a close match, my laundromat in California is not identical to the ones from my Colorado childhood. Here, an old TV bolted in the corner plays Mexican music shows and telenovelas. A few East Indian couples wash their clothes, but most customers are Mexican. The men wear embroidered belts with elaborate metal belt buckles. A young boy runs his remotely operated car through my feet. An older boy, maybe thirteen, chubby and handsome, folds the laundry without being asked. Couples fold together in companionable silence. An older couple—perhaps they run a business together—folds dozens of white towels.

I'm happy to be folded in with these noisy machines and quiet people. Still, the degree of my peace puzzles me, especially as I have no special love, generally, of machines, noises, crowds, or household chores. Then I realize. Just recently, I have lost someone I love. A dear friend, far too young. Again, in the presence of death, I find myself in a laundromat in a suspended state in between too many obligations, where I have nothing but a simple task in front of me.

In the presence of death, when my brain melts and my heart bruises, I need a job. I need something to do with my hands. I need that rattley noise to drown the cluttered chatter of my mind. I need to be with people who smile shyly but demand nothing. Grief is a

In Praise of Inadequate Gifts

water balloon I've been carrying in my chest, and I move carefully to keep it from breaking over those I love or dampening all that work I still have to do. But here, to the sound of the water sloshing in machines, I can slowly release my watery sadness. It fills my body evenly, a sweet and vibrating ache.

Maybe I need to believe in cycles. Night and day. Death and birth. Dirty laundry and clean. Sheets in a dryer, round and round. Maybe I need to believe in a larger order: the round token goes in the round hole; the shirts go with the shirts; and I fit, too, in the little cave of my life. Maybe when the weight of grief makes me so weak I don't know how I will walk into tomorrow, these rhythms, louder and stronger than my own, will carry me.

III.

FAITHFUL OVER A FEW THINGS

Every week I visit Faye, age ninety-two. We've been friends for thirteen years. For the first ten, she was my next-door neighbor on a sweet street of houses built in the thirties and forties and shaded by large sycamores. For the last three years—since I left my husband behind in the little gray duplex whose windows overlook Faye's rose-laden fence—I drive twenty minutes from the neighboring town for our weekly evening of chatting and bad television.

We have little in common: not our age or history or passions. So why do I go?

Not because I want to cling to my old life. I don't want to return to my former neighborhood and be reminded of the sadness of a long, failed marriage, to see the old details I'd loved, standing just as they were when I'd left them: The silvery cherry tree in the front yard. The blue paint flaking from the trim of the picture window. The profusion of star jasmine pouring over the low brick wall. The big weeds my ex-husband won't pull from the patio because they blossom into purple flowers in the summer.

I also have to face the neighbors watering their lawns or walking their dogs. At first, they didn't seem to know whether to ignore me, just wave, or speak. We'd been a pleasant, reliable couple, so the breakup was a shock to us all. My stoic, contractor husband started to cry all the time, which disconcerted everyone who saw him. And then there was the rumor started by Millie across the street, who sees everything through that crack in her curtain, about that man who helped me move my boxes. I smile and greet the neighbors and cheerfully ask about their pets and jobs and children. Finally, after three years of my regular visits, the strain has eased from their faces, but most conversation is still embarrassingly stiff.

Not because I have spare time. I'm a busy high school teacher, and my unscheduled moments are my most valuable resource. I ration them carefully.

Not because Faye is a lesson in how to live a long life. My parents died relatively young. My father's mother, the one I'm said to resemble, died in her nineties. I want to know how to live a long life—or, at least, how to live well. So I read the newspaper articles, magazines, and books with the newest conclusions: no alcohol, except a daily glass of red wine with a meal; a diet low in saturated fats; regular exercise; participation in a religious community (whether the benefits come from the religion or the community, the scientists can't discern); an active social circle; a meaningful way to contribute to society. New research suggests that slightly under eating lengthens life—although I think I'll reject that particular advice. A long life span seems, also, to run in the genes.

It's true, Faye doesn't eat much, and before her son hired her caretakers, she subsisted on cheap preservative-stuffed danishes from Walmart. Before that, when she was still mobile, she'd carry a tray of home-baked cookies and cupcakes to my house in her bright red polyester pants. In her late eighties she was hospitalized several times, and after each hospitalization, a physical therapist would come to her house for three free sessions of exercises. Faye was charmed by the earnest young therapists, but a few weeks after their last visit, she'd return to her sedentary ways. She refuses my offer to drive her to the community center; most of her friends have died, and she claims not to know anyone there anymore. She can't get up the stairs at her church, but she won't let me take her to the stairless church just a block away. Her social circle has been reduced to her neighbors, a friend and a few relatives who occasionally call, and, most recently, the Ethiopian women who care for her four hours a day.

Years ago I asked Faye the secret to a long life, and she answered, "A sense of humor. Laugh a lot." And she does, with a real old-lady cackle. She told me she and her longest-lived sister—who once mailed her a chamber pot as a gag—laughed the most in their pack of siblings. But lately, Faye has unaccustomed bouts of sadness. Remembering her siblings, she said to me again the other night, "I'm the last one left." And yet she lives. And lives. Even when she shakes her fist at "the man in the sky" and tells him she's tired and ready to go.

Not because Faye is living history. I'm one of those rare specimens who actually enjoy other people's home movies and vacation slideshows. At a party you might find me in the corner with someone's grandparent, listening to rambling stories of the olden days. But the past doesn't much interest Faye. When we watch television, I try to steer her away from the true crime and reality shows toward the black-and-white movies, which might remind her of her youth. She'd rather watch *Dr. Phil* or *Entertainment Tonight* or any sitcom with a loud laugh track.

Only through years of listening carefully and catching the rare dropped detail can I begin to glimpse where Faye sits in the flow of American cultural history. She was born on a farm near Joplin, Missouri, the seventh of thirteen siblings. Her father liked to laugh and play the piano, but with so many offspring, he was benignly neglectful. She attended school in a one-roomed schoolhouse and adored her teacher.

When Faye first got sick about five years ago, she was suddenly awash in memories of the Dust Bowl years, during which her family boarded up the farmhouse windows, and still the wind drove grit through the cracks, covering everything inside. In her near delirium in the hospital, she asked to read "that book." I brought her *The Grapes of Wrath*, pleased she wanted something other than the large print-version of *Reader's Digest*. But sure enough, as soon as her health began to improve, her Dust Bowl memories, along with her longing to read, receded.

Faye moved to the San Francisco Bay Area more than sixty years ago—to what is now Silicon Valley—when the land was still covered in orchards. Her husband got a managerial job at the Libby's fruit processing plant, where Faye worked the line, pulling out bad peaches and apricots. They moved into their newly constructed house in Mountain View and watched the neighborhood transform from humble, middle class residences flanked with agricultural fields, to a blue-collar town squeezed by strip malls with old muscle cars jacked up in driveways, to today's upscale community where the land is worth three times the value of the homes and high-tech executives scoop up and painstakingly remodel the aging bungalows. But Faye never speaks of the rapid change of her valley. Her only complaint: Strawberries don't taste as good as they used to.

Not because Faye will give me her story. Faye collects teacups, which she keeps in a glass cabinet in her dining room. Her neighbor Millie collects pink furniture and mouse, frog, and elephant figurines. I collect personal stories. My bookshelves are overflowing with memoirs and hundreds of my own journals. When I meet new people, I search for their central defining narrative: a life-transforming event; a driving passion; a trauma; a rope-tight tie to a person, place, or idea; a vocation; a hope or a terrible fear—whatever it is that pulses within them and forms their life into its particular shape.

I try to find Faye in her house, with its wood paneling so popular in the seventies; the lacy pink fan on her wall; her decorative wooden telephone like the one from her childhood; her musty floral couch with the hand-crocheted polyester throws; the year-round Christmas figurines like the ceramic mouse in a Santa hat; the framed, fading elementary-school photographs of her grandchildren, now grown and with children of their own. A note from her favorite great granddaughter, who no longer visits, taped on her fridge for fifteen years. It reads, "I love you Grandma."

I try to find Faye in her likes and dislikes: Her favorite color is red. Her favorite bird is the cardinal, that bright flash from her childhood. She likes nuts but can't digest them. Same with garlic. In fact, she's always had a sensitive stomach. She likes hot chocolate, but not chocolate candies. Her favorite pies are custard and banana cream. Her favorite cookies are Walker's Scottish shortbreads, which I buy her almost every week. She loves anything made primarily of butter, sugar, and flour. But she doesn't eat much. She's barely over five feet tall, and slight, but she doesn't like to be called "little." She doesn't care for football or basketball, but likes NASCAR races.

Faye and I do not—as I do with my other women friends—put our heads together over tea and analyze our childhoods and our love lives. Faye came of age in an era when hardworking farm women didn't have the luxury of dissecting the subtleties of their parents' childrearing decisions or monitoring the delicate ebb and flow of emotions; there was urgent, physical work to be done and crop failures and disease and death.

So I can't push Faye toward the deeper stories. For one, her short-term memory is getting fritzier, so that now she might ask me three times in five minutes, "How are you?" "How's work?" She tells me the same stories about the neighbors from week to week: "Millie's having trouble walking." "That couple gave their little dog away." "Judy goes to chemo now. It's painful, she says, and she looks awful, but she still takes good care of those children." I make the same acknowledging sounds I do every week. But the repetitions circle only her current life. Her long-term memories remain mostly intact, a great untapped well. When I try to access them with my questions, I usually hit dry dirt. But if I listen long enough, memories bubble up of their own accord, one detail at a time, pushed by a reference on TV or, just as often, by some internal shift I can't see.

Faye has one foot that is shrunken and twisted so that she has to walk on her toes. I guessed polio, but it was some other childhood sickness that lodged itself in her leg and destroyed her fantasy of being a tap dancer. In her town there was a "colored" boy her age who used to tap-dance for money on the street. She wanted to be like him.

When Faye's husband, Glen, was sixty, he died of a heart attack. Almost every day, she'd baked him the pies he loved, so when she learned what contributes to heart disease, she blamed herself.

Not long after his passing, her daughter, only forty, died of lung cancer. Three years ago, her granddaughter, who had two children and suffered from depression, died of an overdose of prescription medications. Just this year Faye's sister—her favorite sibling and the last one living—died.

And then this: We were watching *Dr. Phil* as he harangued some bad husbands. Suddenly Faye turned to me and said, "Glen never told me he loved me."

I had never before heard her say anything disparaging about her husband. "That must have been painful, Faye."

"And he slept with my sister. The alcoholic one." There is a sharp, uncharacteristic hurt in her voice.

I was stunned, this news having burst forth so unexpectedly. I sat in the sadness with her, not knowing what else to say.

"That must have made you feel so sad."

"It did."

Not because visiting Faye is an obligation or a habit. Over the years, there is much I have done from habit or duty, but, since the death of my parents and my divorce, I'm apt to hold every object and activity to the light and examine it for its usefulness. I've donated dozens of overstuffed boxes to Goodwill, resigned from committees, and withdrawn from cluttering relationships. Nothing stays in my life unless it's essential. So Faye must be essential.

Not because Faye is my ideal grandmother. When I was a kid, I had a vision of the grandmother I should have: The matriarch of a historic house on the coast of Maine, where a gaggle of school-aged cousins could stay all summer, tumbling over one another like puppies. She was an intellectual with loose-fitting clothes and wild hair who presided over dinner conversations that flowed from politics to philosophers to modern art. Under our wise grandmother's watch, my cousins and I would be free from judgment and expectations, our minds blooming like the wildflowers surrounding the house.

What I really had was this: A single mother, gripped by mental illness that kept her full of rage, estranged from her family, and constantly moving around the Front Range of Colorado. An ex-hippie father with unfulfilled dreams of getting a doctoral degree whom I visited during the summer in Canada and whose own sadness made him more and more withdrawn. A younger sister. And grandparents I rarely saw.

So Faye resembles neither my fantasy nor my actual family. But perhaps Faye and I are becoming family. (I'm reminded of the Oscar Wilde line: "To lose one parent may be regarded as a misfortune; to lose both looks like carelessness." And although I know the deaths are not my fault, I can't help but feel there is something flawed about me to have lost so much.) Before I leave Faye's house each week, she kisses me on the cheek and says, "I love you like you were my own daughter." The statement is both true and not true. Faye didn't raise me, and she can't hold in her mind the details of my history or even my daily life, but the affection that rises in her is real, as is my affection for her. We try to name it, and "family" is as close as we can come.

In Praise of Inadequate Gifts

Not because Faye is my community service project. I send monthly donations to charitable organizations, participate in events for my friends' causes, and assure myself that teaching, with all its unpaid hours, *is* community service. Still, I feel guilty I don't do more. My friends are reliably impressed that I visit Faye. "Your former next-door neighbor? You visit her every week?" they ask, as if it were a charitable act.

In college, I read a line in Thoreau's *Walden*: "If I knew for a certainty that a man was coming to my house with the conscious design of doing me good, I should run for my life." This turned my sense of service on its head. I asked myself who had truly assisted me in my life and realized that, in the chaos of my childhood, the people who helped me most hadn't been aware of my pain at home: the eighth-grade teacher who asked me to be an aide in the class for the hearing impaired; the high school English teacher who demanded high quality work from me and once nominated me to represent our school in an essay contest. They helped me by believing I had something to give.

This I know: If I visit Faye only because I pity her or feel obligated to her, I will be of no service at all.

Not to earn karma points. In the years of Faye's mysterious and debilitating health issues, when I was still her neighbor, the hospital would often release her before she was well enough to fully function on her own. I'd spend the night on an air mattress in her hallway so I could help her to the bathroom. Neighbors did her shopping. My husband assisted with her bills.

Watching Faye, I began to fear disability in my own old age. I have no children. My retirement accounts are modest. Although I have a new love, I have no guarantee of a partner at the end of my life. Once after a torrent of panic, I comforted myself by thinking that maybe by visiting Faye, I was depositing end-of-life-care points in a karmic account. But as quickly as the thought came, I dismissed it. I know little of the intricacies of karma, but life has taught me this much: The good I do from a place of genuine love and generosity and without a balance sheet, always returns to me. And this I also know: There is no formula I can discern, no tidy one-to-one correspondence between what I give and receive, no neat trick to escape future suffering.

Not because Faye is a guru. My friend and fellow English teacher Marc asked me why I visit Faye. "She's wise?" he guessed. "She gives you good advice?"

I remembered Faye's most recent complaint: "There are too many Black people on TV." (At first she had called Barack Obama "That Black Guy," and then, because she couldn't remember his name, "Boo-Boo." And then she voted for him.)

"No," I said. "Not really."

Marc asked a few more questions, and I answered awkwardly and vaguely. Marc finally concluded, "It's a rest for you, being with her."

In a sense, he's right. My schedule is full, and I compulsively try to improve myself by setting goals, eating right, exercising, and using every moment productively. My visits with Faye are a pause, existing in a slower time zone.

Faye reminds me to be in the present moment. Like a Zen nun, she doesn't mull over the past or plan for the future. She doesn't define herself by her education, achievements, connections, or possessions. Her attention to the present, though, doesn't come through philosophical training. Her now-ness arises from a combination of her upbringing, her native personality, and the demands of her age. With her health and memory issues, she can't impose her will on the future, fulfill new ambitions, or heal the past by ruminating on it. This isn't mysticism: it's being ninety-two.

But being with Faye is not always restful. Some days she's exhausted, and the contagious weariness soaks into my bones. On her more muddled days, conversation is a struggle for us both. She'll ask the same question over and over, and I'll have to decide which details to repeat while trying to keep my tone fresh.

I've learned the hard way that I must be careful about what I tell Faye: disturbing stories get stuck in loops in her mind. Several years ago, she heard on the news that a student from my school, walking home, had been kidnapped and sexually assaulted before she escaped from the back of the car several towns away. When Faye asked

In Praise of Inadequate Gifts

me about it, still raw with my own grief, I told her the girl was my student. Every week for the next six months, Faye worried over her: "How's that girl?" Always, she remembered the attack, but never my updates about her steady recovery, the money the PTA had collected for her, or how she'd started community college.

I now monitor what I say to Faye. I try not to infantilize her—I want our friendship to be based on honesty—yet I don't want her mind revisiting some instance of suffering she has no power to ease. So, for the most part, I don't ask her to carry my sorrows with me. We generally keep to small talk and then watch TV turned up mind-rattlingly loud. Sometimes I make Faye hot chocolate or we eat cookies or dessert breads. During the blasting commercials, we turn toward each other and smile or laugh about nothing, or Faye tells me something she just remembered. "When I was a girl, my family made me in charge of making the ice cream." And it *is* a break, really, to sit next to each other yelling out the answers to *Are You Smarter Than a 5th Grader?* and admiring the routines on *So You Think You Can Dance.*

Not because Faye teaches me how to face death. Before I met Faye, I knew little of what it meant to grow old. All my grandparents died far from me, before I saw significant signs of their deterioration. My father died seven years after his diagnosis and, in his stubborn solitude, hid his suffering, kept his end-of-life thoughts to himself, and allowed no one to care for him until the last possible moment. I hadn't known my mother was ill until she asked my sister and me to visit, just a week before her death. Her bones showed through her skin. All the expressions I'd ever seen her make flitted over that emaciated, hollow face. And then she was gone.

I want to know what it's like at the end of a life, when you measure your future, not in decades, but in years or months. But, for the most part, Faye's thoughts do exactly what mine do: buzz around in their orbit of habitual day-to-day concerns. She worries about her neighbor's chemotherapy. She complains that her Ethiopian in-home aides can't cook American food. She wants a new armchair with the hydraulic lift, because pulling herself up to her walker has become an ordeal. If she had the money, she'd replace the mint-colored carpet she's had since the sixties. Millie's legs have been hurting, but now she's going for a daily walk again. And have I seen how tall Daniel next door is getting? He's going to high school next year. We do not speak of death.

In the hospital with a serious illness, Faye, in that frail, small body, will fight vigorously for her life. But, later, when she gets a touch of the flu, she wails, "Why won't God take me?" Usually her fears settle, not on her own death, but on being forced to leave her home. "They'll have to take me out of here feet first," she says.

When Faye was ninety, she stopped driving Tammy Tomato, the little red Ford Tempo I'd given her, because she backed it into my ex-husband's car and wasn't aware of it until he told her later. By that point she could no longer bend over to pick up things she had dropped. She was having trouble cooking, but wouldn't accept Meals on Wheels. Her legs were frighteningly thin, and she fell down so often, the paramedics made keys to her house. Doing laundry one day, she tripped in the garage and hit her head on the fire extinguisher, spraying fire retardant everywhere. The paramedics— "They're so nice"— whisked her to the hospital, and I spent an afternoon cleaning powder off of every imaginable surface.

So Faye's son Bud, already in his seventies, flew her to Alabama to live with him and his cheerful wife, six little dogs, cable TV, and Sunday after-church BBQs. But Faye talked her way back to her own house in California. Bud hired attendants for four hours a day, which isn't enough, but more than she'll admit she needs. Her mobility has slowly decreased, but her health has steadied, with no more falls or mysterious pains that land her in the hospital. She seems content.

Another of my elderly friends, a therapist who knew she was dying, read books on dying well, met with her clients until her last months, and invited everyone she loved for quiet visits at her bedside, which she had surrounded with flowers. She designed her own memorial service with her favorite Christian, Buddhist, and Sufi prayers and music by Bach. Perhaps we all die just as we live: gracefully, awkwardly, in wisdom, and in ignorance. Perhaps Faye holds no secrets about how to face my own end.

But I do feel differently now about the elderly. When you know a very old person, underneath their wrinkles you can see the faces of all their other ages, held in place by the shape of the bone. I remember my grandmother once checking her lipstick in the rearview mirror and saying, "That face always surprises me. I'm always the same age inside." Faye laughs so easily, she makes the changes of her aging body seem like a joke. A costume. She seems astounded sometimes as she says, "I'm an old lady." Then she cackles.

I used to say, watching two elderly women crossing the streets in flowered hats, holding each other's arms: "Look at those cute old ladies." I didn't mind the stereotypes that pepper movies and television shows. Now, old people are no longer cute or mean or silly or wise to me. They are people, in all their broken fullness. Despite glitches in faculties and functioning, anyone who's lived that long has learned something I don't know.

When Faye was in the hospital with her joints aching, her nose bleeding, and bile in her mouth, the physicians took an MRI and looped miniature cameras through her digestive system. A young doctor with a clipboard diagnosed her, in a flat, dismissive voice, "She's just old." The hospital sent her to a convalescent home where she was expected to die. I wanted to scream at her doctors, "What if she was your grandmother?" And "Someday you'll be her age!" Finally, through the care of wiser doctors and the enigmatic process of healing, she found herself well enough to leave her hospital bed and return home for another five years.

Maybe because she is there. I heard an interview on the radio once with a professor who had a proximity theory of romantic love. According to his studies, the most common cause of romantic love is proximity. You fall in love with those nearby: At your workplace, your gym, your antique-car club. In your neighborhood.

Maybe because, in each other's presence, we can feel. I cry regularly at Faye's, usually during episodes of *Grey's Anatomy*, which Faye calls "that doctor show." She can't remember the characters from week to week, nor follow the convoluted plots. Faye sits next to me. She doesn't look at me and then she does, and I don't know if she sees my tears.

Since my divorce and the deaths of my parents, I feel as if a frozen fountain of emotion inside me has defrosted into a watery river. Anything will bring tears to my eyes. A piece of music. Wildflowers on the side of the road. A father walking hand-in-hand with his toddler. Not to mention the suffering of any animal or person anywhere on the planet. My emotions are larger and more physical now, and they wash through me more quickly.

About four months ago, Faye told me she's been crying often. This is new—she's never been a crier—and it worries her. She cried when her neighbor's old black cat died. He was a curmudgeonly creature, slinking through her backyard, hiding behind the tomatoes, pouncing on the songbirds, marking his territory on fences and flowerpots. He'd never let her pet him. But he'd been a regular visitor for fifteen years. I figure she's grieving not only for that reliable life now gone but also for the cat's human who is struggling through cancer.

Faye told me she cried when she watched a news report about a firefighter who died in a massive blaze. She wept during images of the memorial service, when the father was handed his son's helmet. Baffled by her response, she told me, "I don't even know them." Only later did I remember that she, too, is a parent who has lost an adult child.

Six months ago Faye spoke to her doctor about her crying, and he put her on antidepressants. To me, it seems fitting, not a medical problem, for a woman of ninety-two to look back on what has been beautiful, exquisite, or unfulfilled and cry for all her accumulated triumphs and losses; to look forward and see that rest of her life will be, at most, a few years, and cry, because preparing to die is a fear and a relief and a great sadness and maybe the hardest thing she'll ever have to do.

Maybe because we don't judge each other. For many months I didn't tell Faye that my husband and I had separated. I parked on the street and pretended I was trotting over from next door. It was hard enough to carry my own suffering and I wanted to spare her: Faye loves my ex-husband. Before he stopped visiting her, he was the man in her life. He helped her with finances, fixed her porch light, settled her fears. She loved us as a couple, and I didn't want to take that from her.

In Praise of Inadequate Gifts

But Faye already knew. My husband had told her, sobbing on her front porch. She respected my silence for many weeks before finally asking where I was living.

"You're going to get back together?" she asked.

I shook my head.

"I just can't stand to see a grown man cry."

I was silent. I didn't know what was going through her head: the forces of her Christian upbringing and its view of divorce; her own faithfulness to her complicated marriage; her need for a substitute family; the puzzle of our separation, as our marriage had seemed pleasant enough.

She asked, "You're happy?"

I nodded.

"Good. Life is short. You should be happy."

She would repeat the question in the months and years to come. When I answered yes, she would smile widely, flashing her small teeth.

When Faye moved to her son's house in Alabama, I only had a week's notice. I cried, but I was also relieved. In her efforts to stay independent, she had become a weight for the neighborhood. People struggled to help her and still meet the obligations of their own lives. I worried about her falling, her convoluted finances, her transportation, the cleanliness of her house, her nutrition, and her loneliness. At her son's she would be safe.

So when she moved back home several months later, I didn't understand why she'd left home-cooked meals and little dogs and a big family and better television. The only reason I could squeeze out of her: "They're clannish down there." I knew there had to be more, but she couldn't seem to articulate it. I wanted to attribute it to her stubbornness or some kind of denial, but I finally admitted that it wasn't my job to decide where Faye should live and why. So I gave her the same gift she had given me. I just wrapped her in the wish *May you be happy*.

Because I want to know what it means to be faithful over a few things. Sometimes, when I am getting ready to visit Faye and my night is busy and my house is dirty and I'm low on sleep, I'm surprised by a voice saying, "Thou hast been faithful over a few things." The voice is clear and firm and settles my complaints and urges me, against all argument, to go to Faye.

I recognize the line as the first half of a Bible passage: "Thou hast been faithful over a few things; I will make you ruler over many." I can barely grasp how the first half of the passage relates to my visits to Faye, much less figure out how visiting Faye might make me a ruler over something. I do understand this: If I visit Faye primarily for my own gain, our relationship will suffer, just as it will if I visit only for her sake and sacrifice too much of myself. Our moments together must be more than habit, tradition, a tribute to our past. Our relationship must be alive, living and breathing in the present moment.

I feel an undercurrent of guilt for not being equally committed to my wedding-day promise. Is visiting Faye some attempt at repentance, giving to one relationship what I couldn't fulfill in another? By the end of my long marriage, I was wedded primarily to the vow I had made, to the memory of the young man I had met years before, to the history we shared, to the place we occupied in our network of family and friends, to the idea of faithfulness itself. But, all the while, the actual relationship shriveled. I shriveled. My vow had been "until death do us part." A friend once comforted me by saying, "You have died. You can part now."

Faithfulness, in my new, slow beginning, must begin with faithfulness to myself.

Because she let me do right by her. The first time Faye was hospitalized, she fretted over how long her fingernails and toenails were growing. She wouldn't let my husband or the nurses touch her but allowed me to hold her narrow feet. While I clipped and filed her nails, I felt a thread of connection to women all over the world, throughout time, who had cared for other women. In the last few months Faye has needed my help getting into bed. She scoots her walker to the bedside and eases herself onto her too-tall, too-squishy mattress. I gently lift her legs and put them under the covers. Then I adjust her nightgown. With her head nestled on her pillow, her hair a light cloud, she laughs like a little girl. Each time we do this could be the last. I am going to lose Faye, and I sit with her anyway.

I am sorry to see her go, but I feel settled. For once in my life, I know I have done right by someone. I have done right by Faye. But this I know, too. I have done right by Faye because she let me.

Faithfulness begins with faithfulness to ourselves. But that doesn't preclude faithfulness to others, faithfulness that isn't always easy or convenient, faithfulness that strains our schedules and makes us look at death and decay when we want what is shiny and alive. But why my faithfulness to Faye, while I let my husband go? My husband, wrapped as he was in his own long history of emotional troubles, would not allow me to care for him, to be a source of happiness. Faye lets me love her. My love soaks into her, buoys and cheers her. And I let her love me. Our love does each other good.

So maybe our faithfulness is to something bigger: choosing life. For ourselves. For others. Maybe that's the true faithfulness. Maybe with that as our central principle, we will become rulers over the rest.

Only recently has Faye begun to give off the smell of a live body decaying, and when I lean over her, I feel a physical urge to turn away. But I don't. I bend down and press my lips to her cheek, and she kisses me back.

WHY WE DON'T HAVE CHILDREN

Waiting in the cluttered lobby of my car repair shop, I chat with the man across from me on the faux leather couch. He's a round, red-faced, happy grandfather of sixteen grandchildren. We exchange the typical pleasantries of Silicon Valley, comments on the weather and the crazy housing prices, our conversation natural and lilting, until he asks the question—the conversation-stopping one I've been asked hundreds of times since I hit my fertile years.

"Do you have children?"

"No," I answer.

In most casual talk with a near stranger—"Do you like horror movies?" "Are you a football fan?"—a simple yes or no answer is too curt. Social niceties require at least a line or two of explanation, something light and charming—or surprisingly honest, a revelation that creates a sudden intimacy but doesn't burden the listener.

But I don't know what to say, so I don't elaborate.

As usual, he shifts in his seat. Looks to the ceiling and then over my shoulder.

Sometimes I think the questioners fear they've been rude: They imagine the fertility treatments, the miscarriages, the fumbled adoption attempts, a failed marriage, a single life I didn't choose, the child we lost too young. Other times they seem intensely curious, as if they have to will themselves not to ask why. Do I dislike children? Am I too devoted to my career? Does my partner have children from another marriage and won't agree to more?

Finally, the grandfather says, "That's okay."

He's of a smaller group, the ones who feel sad for me. He uses the same tone he'd use comforting his grandson after he'd just lost the game for his baseball team. It means, "This loss is hard, it wasn't my first choice for you, but you'll be alright."

I don't elaborate because, truth is, I'm not sure why I don't have children. I have only guesses, stories I've told myself over the years. And I don't think I'm alone in my bewilderment. A recent *Time*

Magazine article on childless couples cites a Pew study: One in ten women in the 1970s didn't give birth in their lifetimes; now that number is one in five. Many of these women have straightforward explanations. For the rest of us, the reasons are often complex and murky, even to ourselves. So I'm going to try and sort them out, poking around in biology and sociology and psychology, stabbing at religion, peering into my past, sharing secrets I've never told.

We're in denial.

When I was a teenager in the 80s, I saw a character in a movie wearing a T-shirt with "I can't believe I forgot to have children" plastered across her perfect breasts. I remember nothing else from the movie but that shirt, which lodged itself in my mind as something important. Sometime later, when I was in my early twenties, I read a book—which I have also forgotten—in which the author warned of a new trend: women who didn't believe they were aging, who imagined they had infinite time, who surprised themselves by arriving, suddenly, at expensive fertility treatments. Even with the early siren sound, I, too, have been fooled. Now I teeter on the far edge of my fertility, which means, unless I want to adopt or spend a fortune, I've made my choice by not making a choice.

What has caused this mass amnesia? Women are entering challenging careers that take years to establish. We live so much longer, we can't imagine we'd lose our chance to have children not even halfway through our journey. We see media images of women luscious and fertile-looking into their late years. We want to wait to have children until we have time, money, and settled-love, none of which come easily. We are busy plowing the fields of our lives, trudging steadily; we lift our heads for a pause, for a glimpse of the sky, only to find that years have passed as if we were asleep.

We had feminist mothers.

I was raised in the chaos that was called family in the 1970s. Bred on the 1950s ideal that a woman's education was an accessory, my mother felt betrayed when she was left single, without a college degree, trying to find a career that could feed us in a sexist job market. She was filled with feminist rage that kept her relationships with men fleeting and complicated. Our lives might have seemed ordinary to my sister and me, similar as they were to those of our neighbors, if it weren't for our mother's anger over the injustice that was her life—and for television, the sitcom reruns we watched after school while we waited for our mother to come home, all those nuclear families, which made us feel something was wrong with us. Many of my peers emerged from that era of bitter divorce swearing never to marry and never to have children. Even in happy families, mothers warned against having children or having them too young, urging us toward freedoms they never had.

In the midst of my mother's resentments against men and rapidly changing gender roles, I wasn't sure what I should imagine for my own future. I was never the kind of child who daydreamed about my wedding—that sort of play had been stomped out of me by our counter-culture parents who eschewed gendered toys and traditional roles. For a short while in third grade, as I fell asleep, I imagined myself grown and pretty, a handsome man dancing with me—some vague amalgam of fairy tale images—but that lasted only a couple of months before fading.

We're artists.

By sixth grade, I'd cycled through a number of fantasy careers, most enduring of which was being an artist. I visualized myself at the opening of my gallery show. My awkward hair had grown out long and thick and I'd piled it on top of my head in an artistic, messy bun. I wore a long flowing black skirt, and I floated between my paintings, shyly accepting compliments from my admirers.

When I imagined having children, however, I saw myself as a business woman, probably because my mother had recently gotten an office job at an oil company in downtown Denver. I wore a blue business suit, carried a briefcase, and rented a nice apartment. I couldn't picture a man in this scenario, so I'd adopted a daughter. That was as grand a vision of my future as I could conjure: a professionally successful single mother.

Only now do I notice that my artist fantasy doesn't include children while my business one does. Perhaps, even then, I'd absorbed the belief that a successful artist is not a successful parent.

In Praise of Inadequate Gifts

By the time I was in college, I'd abandoned my plans to be a visual artist and had chosen to be a writer instead. I spent my college years into my early twenties fervently debating in my journal whether I could be both a writer and a mother.

Now, the debate seems overly dramatic, even silly. Maybe I've just matured, had decades to recognize the many creative ways there are to build a life. But our culture has changed, too. The model of "writer" has morphed. When I was in college, the writers we met in our canon of great works were generally men, solitary geniuses, sometimes mentally unstable, often cruel or, at best, benignly neglectful of those who loved them. Milton. Tolstoy. Hemingway. Fitzgerald. Their suffering, and that which they inflicted on others, was an unfortunate but necessary cost of their talent.

Now, college students read—and meet—skilled writers of all ages, backgrounds, and gender identification, who have as wide a range of family constellations as any cross section of our culture. Of course, aspiring writers still wrestle with how they will find both money and time to support their work and family, but they have examples of those who have patched together solutions. But for me, scribbling in my journal, the choice felt painfully real.

Did I choose writing over family? Looking objectively at my life, you'd say no. I needed to make a living and chose to be a high school English teacher. It's meaningful work but demanding and exhausting, not a job that releases me to blocks of blissful, productive writing. I carved out what I could. For years, just a half hour a day. Slowly, I created a journaling practice, wrote with my students, took courses, read writing books, joined writing groups—finding cracks of time in my busy days.

If I'd had children, perhaps I'd tell myself that without them, I'd be a writer. I'd underestimate the demands of my childless life. I might not realize how afraid I was, with or without children, to try. The writing in my college journals assumed, should I choose writing over motherhood, I'd make a miraculous leap from my few amateur stories to successful writer. I'd had no idea how much I still needed to learn. In the last couple of years, I've had publications that feel like gifts, but I don't have a body of work that equals the weight of a child.

We need to heal first.

In another way, I did trade a family for writing, not as a career but as healing. I've depicted my mother as a typical, divorced mother of the 1970s, and in many ways she was. But she also suffered from mental health issues, probably borderline personality disorder. Depression kept her locked in her dark room for days, sometimes weeks. Bouts of rage lost her friends and family and jobs. Several times, she flirted with suicide. Her financial issues, combined with a fierce hope that something better waited for her elsewhere, kept her in an endless cycle of new jobs in new towns.

The survival mechanism that got me through my early twenties was to believe my mother's reality: The world had given her a bad rap and I could help by hard work and a positive, cheerful attitude, by intervening for her, by doing for her what she couldn't do for herself. Considering the circumstances, I thought I'd turned out quite well, plucky and reliable. I didn't know how wounded and frightened I was and how writing would help me see truths I'd never face otherwise. I thought writing might be a career; I didn't know it was a path to wholeness or that the work would take decades.

We are perfectionists.

I suspect my childhood experiences are part of the reason I don't have children, although the links are not entirely clear to me. My sister, only two years younger, with an almost identical upbringing, has two boys. Many people with difficult childhoods have courage and faith that they can provide their own children what they were not given; raising their own families can feel like a chance to redeem the past.

Part of my reluctance may be my hyper-vigilant sense of responsibility and over-developed guilt. I once read a psychology article that claimed the person most likely to suffer from over-functioning—or taking too much responsibility for other people's obligations and emotions—is the oldest child in a family of two daughters raised by a single, under-functioning mother. There you go. As I imagined having children, I had impossibly high standards. I must be 100 percent mentally and emotionally present for my children at all times. I must be energetic, stable, consistent. I must be a wise and intuitive guide. I must never make a mistake. Fun, too!

Financial solvency a plus. These are not standards I hold for other parents but when it comes to myself, the knowledge that I will inevitably cause my children to suffer creates so much guilt-in-advance, my only action is delay.

Our current cultural beliefs about child rearing don't help perfectionists. On one hand, our culture—fast-paced and saturated in adult media images—is not child-friendly; on the other hand, never in American history have we been so child-centered. In contrast, my parents, particularly my father, were of the "weeds school of child-rearing": just throw a little water and sunshine at them, leave them alone, and they'll grow up hearty. If you'd asked my dad, he'd say that people have been having children since the beginning of human history—how difficult can it be?

Perhaps in reaction to the weaknesses of the weeds school, we now see children as fragile. Research abounds about the delicate early years, how easily an unskilled parent can damage a child's body, brain, and self-esteem for life. Enter the helicopter parent. In the grocery store, I overhear frightened parents hovering over their temper tantrum-throwing toddler, trying to acknowledge the child's feelings, echoing a script from the latest book. "I know you really wanted that candy. You feel angry because you didn't get that candy. Mommy knows you are angry." In the high school where I teach, some anxious parents text and call their teenagers all day long.

Intellectually, I know the best child-rearing approach lies in the middle way between the weed and helicopter schools. I once read a comforting Buddhist book which promised that children learn to regulate their feelings by watching adults make mistakes, apologize, wrestle with anger and grief, and restore relationships. I believe! I believe! But still, if I were a parent, I know I'd gobble the hundreds of advice books—all written with confident authority, many contradicting each other—wracked with anxiety that whatever I'm doing is causing irreparable damage.

We have jobs working with children.
In the beginning, when someone asked me if I had children, I'd answer, "I'm a teacher."

The questioner would chuckle and say, "You already have so

In Praise of Inadequate Gifts

many kids," or "You have to deal with kids all day."

I *was* parenting, I believed, just broadly. I provided a little bit of parenting to a lot of children for a limited period of time. I've known many female teachers and professors who actively resist—with some anger—those students who try to make parents of them. I don't mind the job. For high school students with absent or dysfunctional parents, I'm happy to attempt to be present and functional. Even teenagers from healthy homes are in the process of separating from their parents and often need some alternative adult connection. The world needs us, the benevolent aunties, I've told myself.

There is some truth to this, yes. And the parenting-in-the-gaps is useful work. If I had my own children, I wouldn't have time or energy to give my students what I do now. But my answer smacks of positive spin. Teaching is a distant relative of parenting, but it is not parenting. Maybe I answered "I'm a teacher" to protect myself from a sense of failure for not having a child, for my inability to accomplish what seems like a rite of passage into adulthood, and from feelings of guilt for not doing the valuable work of raising a family.

We don't have enough time.
And where would I find the time? Recently, I've learned that working mothers today spend more time with their children than the housewives of the '50s and '60s, who devoted their days to cooking and cleaning and visiting neighbors. When the children tumbled home from school, these mothers didn't feel obligated to entertain them but hustled them out the door. For those of my generation and earlier, if we lived in a neighborhood of children, we ran as a feral pack. We devised secret, social hierarchies as frightening as any fraternity and embarked on dangerous adventures complete with injuries we rarely reported, and only scratched our way back home when our parents yelled loudly enough when it was time for dinner. I'm not suggesting we abandon children to their primitive impulses— merely noting that times have changed.

My friends with children devote almost all their free time to their children's activities: dance and music lessons; soccer games and play dates; Scout troops and after-school tutoring; the endless parade of glamorous birthday parties and enriching, educational weekend

In Praise of Inadequate Gifts

activities. At home, they monitor sibling squabbles, enforce practice of the latest skill, help with homework. I can barely manage the most basic demands of my own life—grading papers, folding the laundry, making it to the grocery store so I'm not trying again to invent dinner from the old cans in the back of the cupboard or the mysterious, frost-burned packages at the bottom of the freezer.

Often, I try to imagine how I would fit in a child. How do working parents do it? They do. They are also the most deeply exhausted people I know. I recently stumbled upon another study: a survey of children about their relationship with their parents. The children don't mind so much the parents' long working hours, but they don't like their parents' stress; they wish their parents were happier. I would want my children's childhood, our too-quick time together, to be more than a blur of sad hurry. But I don't know how to make it so.

We don't have enough money.
Money, of course, is an issue. I'm a teacher in Silicon Valley—ranked one of the most expensive places in the nation to give birth and raise a baby—so although my salary is high for the profession, it doesn't keep pace with the escalating cost of living where, recently, rents have almost doubled and where daycare costs would devour half my monthly paycheck. For me, after a childhood of poverty and half my life crawling out of educational debt, I've been enjoying the relief of having enough. Enough underwear. Enough for a movie. Enough to go out to dinner with friends. Most importantly, enough to visit those places in the world I've always wanted to see. I resist returning to not enough.

We're introverts.
However, my teacher friends, who face the same time and money obstacles, continue to have babies. So there must be more to my resistance. Maybe my quiet nature. I'm easily over-stimulated by crowds and noise, and, although not a recluse, need more time alone than the average person. A trip to Costco, with its traffic jam of carts and towering boxes and so many choices, sets my heart racing. Let's be clear: this is not who I want to be. I want to be that woman I love

in the magazines, on TV, who cares for fifteen foster children. She's tired, of course, and the money is tight, but she thrives, too, in this community of her creating, the way all those children need her, how much she knows she has to give, the sense that family is always near. I think she's doing the world's most important work. As much as I want to be her, I've had to accept, reluctantly and through my mistakes, that I'm wired differently. I need moments of slow-time in which to think and understand. To work in a fast-paced, highly interactive job followed by the constant demands of childcare, without quiet pauses, might do me in. I don't want my child-care to be an act of endurance instead of joy.

We don't have support systems.
The research says the happiest parents are ones with extended family nearby who can help with childcare, who can provide those restorative pauses. My parents are dead, the few remaining members of my family scattered.

Our biological clocks are broken.
Or maybe there is something askew with my biology. I don't seem to have the same physical drive to have children as my friends. Yes, I feel a swelling of joy when I hold a newborn, when I catch the eye of a toddler peeking over the back of her chair at a restaurant, when a child nestles against my chest as I read a story aloud. But I've not experienced, as my friends have, that physical longing to carry a baby, an urgency in the muscles and organs. Perhaps I'm damaged, some essential part of myself amputated.

We have bad genes.
Plus, I'm not sure I should be passing on my genes. When I was in my mid-twenties, working at a small alternative school, I asked the teaching team and principal over our daily lunch meeting, "How did you decide you wanted to have children?" I was in search of wisdom, some sign to point me in a direction. My principal, thirty years my senior, seemed surprised. "It wasn't a question when I was young. It's just what we did." I heard in her voice a complicated tone—was I imagining it?—that she was both longing for a simpler time and

contemplating what her life might have been had she realized she had choices. But then her mind snapped shut, her small, fine-featured face hardened with certainty, and she answered in her preachy voice. "Back then, those of us who had good genes knew we had a responsibility to pass them on." I was surprised by her Darwinian answer—and her confidence in the superiority of her genes. At that time, I'd only framed my question metaphysically and emotionally: What's my life purpose? Is having children part of that purpose? Am I emotionally well enough to be a good mother?

I thought my principal's argument was classist and overly proud. But, truth be told, her comment terrified me. My great-grandfathers on both sides had each murdered someone in a fit of rage. My father, although quite bright, seemed to have frightening warps in his memory and live in a fuzzy universe of his own creating. Both my sister and I are anxious and overly sensitive, prone to obsessive thoughts. Most of all, I feared I'd give birth to a child like my mother. My mother's hell—her paranoia and rage and depression and restlessness and loneliness—was not a state of consciousness I'd bestow on anyone. I'd be doing the world a favor to cut off my line.

It's immoral to bring children into a world that will cause them suffering. Early in my marriage, when I was still in the throes of processing my childhood, my father startled me by pronouncing, "You should have a kid." I thought it odd advice from a man who, as a father, seemed to suffer and cause so much suffering. Three marriages. Three biological daughters and one adopted. Court cases and angry ex-wives and children who felt abandoned and misunderstood. At the time, my response was visceral. Childhood was too hard. I agreed with Schopenhauer who argued that, in a human life, pain always outweighs joy; therefore, we should not bring children into this world only to gift them with a few fleeting moments of happiness and a lifetime of suffering.

I didn't realize my view had changed until a conversation with my mother-in-law half way through my marriage. I knew my mother-in-law wanted grandchildren—I'd stumbled upon the little clothes and toys squirreled away in her attic, seen her face when her friends subjected her to endless photos of their progeny. She never pressured

In Praise of Inadequate Gifts

me, but I felt guilty I hadn't given her that gift. So she surprised me one afternoon at the end of a lunch together. Out of the blue, she said, "I understand why you don't have children. I wouldn't bring children into this world either. It's so different now than when my children were small." I murmured something brief and affirming, glad for her empathy, but as soon as she'd said it, I knew that was no longer a reason for me.

Yes, as a teacher in the Bay Area, I've thought much about the challenges of raising children in my community: the pace, stress, competition, consumerism, income disparity—the pressure, too young, to be an adult. But I don't believe life is worse for children today than in the past. Children have always suffered, although the forms change. But for me now, the daily joys, their ordinariness and depth and brilliance, are worth a spin on this earth.

Population growth is bad for the planet.

In my college environmental studies class my freshman year, we studied the population crisis. Our professor, a wiry, energetic man shaped by the idealism of the '60s, tried valiantly to inspire us to environmentally responsible action. He'd chosen not to have children as a political and moral statement. His wife, younger than him, with a soft round face, longed for a baby but would not fight his energetic righteousness.

With all the passion of a freshman, I wanted to support the health of the planet, but I felt uneasy about his stand. Intellectually, I understood his anti-child argument. I could also argue the other side: What if his unborn child would develop a vaccination for malaria or a cheap desalination machine or a cost-effective solar car, or anything that would serve humanity? My discomfort wasn't intellectual but emotional. Some people, like my professor's wife who mothered all of us, seemed to have a calling to have children, a deep yearning, something essential to their nature. Who was I to argue she should sacrifice that desire—or that her longing wasn't in service of a divine purpose?

Having children is not our fate.

Maybe the belief that most of us even have a choice is illusion. The

In Praise of Inadequate Gifts

ancient Greeks—and a host of religions before and since—believe in fate: the major events of our lives are predestined, marriages and births and deaths all written by the hand of some divine scribbler. If so, I am relieved from my questioning, my confusion, my self-blame. I've not failed to craft a life or shape my character into one that can support a family but am, instead, living my destiny. It's not my fault.

Problem is, I don't really believe it.

Yet there are moments when I feel some power larger than chance or biology at work in the creation of families. One of my favorite college professors told me that not long before she got pregnant with both her son and daughter, she felt them as a presence, almost as if they were hovering over her shoulder, whispering, waiting. She had a clear sense of their identities, already in existence, ready to join her. Just recently, a friend, a mother of two small children, said to me, "When I look in my children's eyes, I feel as if they were meant to be mine." A biologist might argue that her hormones cause her bond with her children; their shared genes make her children seem familiar to her. But my friend, well-educated and leaning toward the agnostic, feels something larger, the sense that her children are more than their little bodies. They have a spiritual identity and—in some larger pattern she can't discern with her limited human perceptions—have come to rest in her family. I can't deny that when my friend and professor spoke with warm eyes, not out of any religious doctrine, but in awe of the mystery, I believed them. I believed them.

I've never heard an unborn child whispering over my shoulder. I *have* had dreams: I've given birth to kittens, several times. I had a child and forgot her, left her behind at the grocery store. Before I was married, I dreamed, most vividly, that I gave birth to a baby who was instantly a toddler, serene and wise, with dark wavy hair and blue eyes, who could already talk in complete sentences. So when I married a man with dark hair and blue eyes, I thought I'd dreamed my own little girl. But we never had children and then we divorced. Does this mean that no children ever knocked? Or have I been willfully deaf, so they have floated on to some more receptive door?

We are avoiding our destiny.

Many years ago, I went for a run at a local nature preserve. As I paused at the water fountain near the organic farm, an old man wobbled up behind me on a bicycle. Unlike the regulars with their slick gear, he rode a creaky bike and wore a faded flannel shirt. He stopped beside me and made a few cheerful comments about the park. He had a wrinkled brown face, deep brown eyes, and black hair that belied his age—the very stereotype of wisdom from a cheesy TV movie. Then, without any context, he stared into my eyes and told me firmly, "Having children is the most important thing you will ever do. You have to have children. You'll always regret it if you don't." He turned and teetered away in puffs of dust. What? Who has a wise man on a bicycle appear out of thin air and command her to have a child? How could I, who was always looking for signs, ignore him?

Part of me did believe I was destined to have a child . . . a mentally ill or addicted one. The Powers That Be had chosen me to serve those who suffer. My sacrifice to my mother's consuming needs—time, attention, money, relationships, even my sense of reality—was boot camp training for a lifetime appointment. I'd been chosen to aid the anguished, an assumption reinforced by my assortment of friends and closest students wrestling with mental illness. I'd accept my calling of serving such a child—it was a noble duty, a sacred trust—but I didn't feel ready. I just wanted a little more time. Just a little more time. Just a little more time.

We were mothers in our past lives.
Once, while driving away from dinner at my mother-in-law's house, again feeling guilty for not giving her grandchildren, I had a sudden vision. I'd already been a mother. In my past life. Many lives. Of big families. I didn't know if I actually believed in past lives, but in my vision I saw a fuzzy image of a dented metal pot over a kitchen fire. A long brown dress with a cream-colored apron tied around my waist. Children at my feet and in the fields. That explained what felt like memories of long days cooking and cleaning, mending and tending. I'd done my duty.

And (bonus!) this belief promised I hadn't missed my chance. I had many more lifetimes to be a mother again. I was just sitting out this round. I basked for almost a week in the sweet relief of this revelation. Then, while driving the highway between home and work,

In Praise of Inadequate Gifts

the thought occurred to me that a therapist might explain my sense of past lives, tell me that I hadn't been a mother in a previous incarnation but in my own childhood, taking care of my mother. My relief dissolved again into uncertainty.

We are will-less water droplets.

Or maybe we are not governed by destiny or biology or psychology. Maybe all of humanity is part of one great social body, and like cells, we each have a job assigned to us. Think ants and bees: a few reproduce for the group while the rest are barren workers and warriors. Think of the California sheephead: all fish are born female but some morph into males when the need arises. Think of the clownfish, which are all male until the breeding female dies and the largest male transforms into the next mom. They are not making individual choices but serving the community, a single shared mind.

After I divorced, I fell in love with a younger man. Several years into the relationship, I read an article, "All the Single Ladies," in *The Atlantic* by Kate Bolick. She noticed an increase in the number of women dating younger men and linked the trend to economic changes: As women gain more financial independence and power, they no longer need men for security or status; they can choose, instead, to prioritize their emotional needs. For the same reasons, women now feel more comfortable dating shorter men. Bolick cites a study that finds "a 40 percent increase, between 1986 and 2003, in men who are shorter than their wives." My emotionally satisfying younger boyfriend is also shorter than me. At first, I was a little proud to be on the forefront of the latest trends—finally, some evidence that I'm cutting edge—but then I became disoriented. I'd imagined I was making my own choices, but maybe I'm just a will-less water droplet riding the crest of a cultural wave.

And then, suddenly, all my meditations on children, which feel so urgent and personal, seem but a snapshot, a narrow slice of time and place in human history, a short braid of religion and economics and gender roles gathered in a document, *Contemporary Portrait: Silicon Valley,* already being tucked away into an archive, already sliding into the past.

We're too smart to have children.

Statistics predict that the more educated a woman, the older she'll be at the birth of her first child and the less likely she'll have a child. The higher her IQ, the less likely she is to give birth. Smart people don't have kids, a kind person pointed out to me, thinking I'd find it affirming. But as much as I value intelligence, I don't equate it with wisdom. Smart people may lean too heavily on their clever brains, to which the acquisition of a time-consuming, resource-gobbling, stress-inducing, financial-suck of a baby will never be logical; they may not be listening to their intuition, which discerns gifts the logical brain may never compute.

I suspect my brain likes to keep itself thinking to avoid feeling. It pokes around the edges of a topic to distract itself from a primitive pain crouching at the center.

We have bad marriages.

Maybe you've guessed I've left some things unsaid. I've kept some secrets. All my philosophical prattling about fate and free will, mutterings over money and time have, hiding under them, a simpler truth. I spent the length of my childbearing years in a bad marriage. Sure, some of our obstacles to having children were external—money, time, housing—but the biggest block, I can now see, was our relationship. I didn't know it at the time: I'd married young, I had few models of healthy relationships, and we drifted so slowly into our marital sickness. And I ignored the hints. About five years into my marriage, I confessed to my sister I didn't think I could bring a child into our home, into the dynamic of our relationship. "Why would you stay in a relationship that isn't good for a child?" she said. "Aren't you as important as a child?" I couldn't hear her wisdom. Instead, I blamed myself for my inability to create a life that could support a child.

We are rotten inside.

Here is another secret, one I've never told anyone. I thought I was rotten inside. Over the years, many people have spontaneously told me I'd make a good mother. I'd bashfully thank them for what, to me, is a great compliment. But I didn't believe them. I knew I appeared right enough on the outside, and I didn't fear I'd verbally or physically abuse my children. But, for the length of my marriage, I believed that in the very core of my being, like the dead center of an old tree, was hidden decay. Dark. Messy. Irreversible. My children would never see it, but I'd taint them. I couldn't allow them near that decay.

We are afraid of intimacy with our children.
Here is my most shameful secret: I didn't want to be pregnant because I didn't want to be that physically close to another human being. Most of my friends longed for a chance to wrap their whole body around their growing baby. The image made me feel invaded, devoured, claustrophobic.

We're exhausted by our imaginary children. (Wait, I think that's just me.)
Here is my most peculiar secret. Several years ago, I developed a habit, so deeply ingrained I didn't recognize its oddness. I began living a double life. Many times during my demanding work days I would imagine, in full and wearying detail, that I was raising children. Usually two. Their ages varied, but usually they lingered in their toddler years, that particularly demanding time. Mornings, I'd mentally get us all ready and out the door: gathering snacks and backpacks and lost shoes. Evenings, I'd try to do my schoolwork and still give my children time and attention, feed them well, keep up with laundry and cleaning . . . and so much time on the bedtime routines. I read parenting magazines with their tips for quick, healthy snacks and settling sibling squabbles. What probably began as a simple question about how my life might change if I had children became an obsessive loop in which, for several years, I was living my actual life plus an imaginary one.

I think it was a kind of penance for not having the same struggles as my hard-working parent friends. Of course my imaginary life was not as wearing as being a real parent, but it burdened me. It was not until I mentioned my imaginary children—as a random aside—to a friend and saw her expression that I realized my habit was strange, and, more importantly, a weight I could choose to set down. I have said goodbye to my imaginary children. It was easier than I thought.

We like our lives.

Several years ago, not long after my parents' deaths and my divorce, I realized, to my great surprise, that I no longer had a rotting center. My insides were fresh and clean. What was the decay and where had it gone? Had it evaporated with my losses? Was it my own anger I couldn't admit to myself? Was I carrying the darkness of those I loved because it was too big for them to carry it themselves—or because I didn't know how to avoid absorbing it?

Not long after I met my younger man, I was also shocked to discover I could imagine carrying a child—and the thought was joyful. Perhaps my resistance to holding another being inside me was related to my pattern in relationships, the way I habitually compromised too much of myself to appease and please. In my past the only place that belonged to me—where I had no demands to accommodate but my own—was my private interior world. I was afraid of a hungry baby living there. Maybe with more room for myself in my life, I was no longer afraid to share my body.

My boyfriend and I probably could have had children had we skipped the leisurely get-to-know-you stage and tumbled right into family. But I was still healing from my losses, learning to trust my new life. He was starting a new career. "You can always adopt!" cheerful-hopeful people say, rooting for me. And then I have to admit to myself my final secret, the one I find it hard to admit because I fear it means I'm selfish: I like my life. It isn't the one new parents imagine they're missing: nightly lovemaking, candlelit dinners, spontaneous weekend trips, a movie any night of the week. But I like having time to exercise most days. I like peaceful mornings and time to think and chances to travel. I like being able to give attention to my partner and students and friends. I'm a bit of a workaholic, but my life is rich in quiet pleasures.

Maybe I've kept my mind occupied with the busy work of raising my imaginary children and rehearsing the well-worn list of my character weaknesses because I can't bear to think about what I've missed. I've consciously tried not to be one of those women-without-children who can't attend a baby shower or befriend a pregnant woman. But if I'm honest, I admit that I also grieve. Mostly, I mourn quietly enough I

In Praise of Inadequate Gifts

can ignore the sound, but sometimes, when I'm not expecting it, I hear a distant, lonely howl.

Here's a selfish reason I want children: I believe being a parent forces personal and spiritual growth. Whether or not you want it, parenting slams you up against your own childhood, the choices your parents made with you, the legacies you'll choose to keep and abandon, your weaknesses . . . your belief you have control over anything. Childrearing is a master course in ego-shredding—which I think is necessary for enlightenment—one I'm not sure any other experience can replace. But more fundamentally, all parents I know say they never really understood love until they had a child. I want to love that large, that fiercely, that unconditionally. I want to watch my child sleep and feel my heart ache with tenderness. I want to introduce my child to this world's beauty. Animals. Books. Bright fruit. Dancing. Laughing. Music. Touch. Those are my hungers. Those are my losses.

The woman in the grocery store line, the one with the bright red coat, asks, "Do you have children?"

"No," I say.

The conversation stutters to an awkward pause.

I flip my wrist. "Oh, you know, who has the time these days, am I right?" Or I toss my hair. "Well, you know, I had so many children in my past lives." I grab her wrist and hold her eyes like a woman possessed. "Let me tell you about my mother . . ." "or "I have two imaginary children," or "Have you heard about the clownfish?"

Who can say those things to strangers?

"That's okay," she says, smiling gently.

Yes, I suppose it is. It isn't. And it is.

IN PRAISE OF INADEQUATE GIFTS

When I was in eighth grade, my classmate Patty walked home after school—a sunny Denver, October afternoon—and found her mother in a pool of blood on the kitchen floor, the victim of a random household-robbery-gone-wrong.

Before that day, Patty had been an ordinary junior high school girl. She sat at the far end of the table in my art class and—from what I could see—had average artistic talent. And she was smack in the middle of the popularity ladder: a few close girlfriends but otherwise as invisible as the rest of us, certainly beyond the vision of the glamorous girls and the popular boys who loped after them. I didn't know her well, but occasionally we exchanged words, shy girl to shy girl, as we helped each other with the complicated instructions for our batik wall-hangings of exotic birds.

When the news of Patty's loss hit the front page of the papers, she was no longer invisible. She became That Girl Whose Mother was Murdered. An instant and unprepared celebrity.

Someone thought to buy her a card, to pass it around the school. Students, popular and unpopular, wrote: *if you need anyone . . . I'm here for you . . . I want to be your friend.* Boys in their scratchy hieroglyphics. Girls in their bubbly writing, with hearts or circles dotting their i's and j's. I felt a raw and helpless ache but couldn't find the words to comfort her. I don't remember exactly what I wrote when the card circled around to me, but I do remember feeling my words were as bland and clichéd as the rest.

The day Patty received the card, she sat hunched at the end of my art table, ignoring the crumpled, wax-flaking batik in front of her. She was silent. Seething. The air smelled like melted crayons. Finally she blurted: "*Now* everyone wants to be my friend. Where were they before?"

Just a few bitter words—said to no one, really—but my emotional response was enormous and tangled. I was surprised that in the aftermath of such a catastrophic loss, she was still angry about the social dynamics of our junior high, that even murder hadn't

In Praise of Inadequate Gifts

obliterated the pain of being thirteen and exiled from the in crowd. It was my first lesson in the complexities of grief and trauma.

Later, I would come to understand that the small and ordinary deaths of exclusion and neglect are a form of trauma in themselves. And, more importantly, that shock takes time to integrate. In the beginning, our brain can hold our new reality only a few consecutive moments before it returns to familiar terrain—in Patty's case, her resentment at the popular girls. Where could she throw her anger at such a cosmic injustice but at whomever was nearest?

In retrospect, I also understand that those who cozy up to victims are not always motivated by tenderness. Sometimes we cling to other people's drama because we crave the vicarious adrenaline rush of a life on the edge. We want to sneak toward the places where the veneer of civilization begins to crack, to feel the thrill of impending chaos. Car wrecks. True crime exposés. Maybe that's what Patty sensed in the midst of her wash of unexpected attention. The news cameras turned toward her, and now the popular kids were edging their way into the spotlight.

But at the time, I believed Patty had misunderstood the students who had written in the card, unfairly doubting their sincerity. For me, the murder had obliterated our ridiculous junior high obsessions, had melted the imaginary boundaries that separated us. What did social status matter in the face of such tragedy, one that reminded us of how much we loved our mothers—those same mothers who had, for the last few years, become so intolerably irritating—that reminded us that nothing was more important than caring for each other?

My whole body was a sack of watery grief for Patty. I would have done anything for her, had I only known what she needed. I had added my words to her card, and not only were they vague and meaningless, I had offended her. I had magnified her pain. In the same way that Patty threw her grief onto the popular girls, I tucked my confusion and pain about her loss in my most familiar pocket: guilt and self-blame. And I carried it there, unexamined and unquestioned.

For years after, far into my adulthood, I never sent condolence

In Praise of Inadequate Gifts

cards. I had pushed Patty's story out of my consciousness but had concluded, rather fiercely, that in the face of deep grief, words are inadequate. So I ignored those who were suffering, assuming they knew I was there for them. Likewise, I never imagined that I, who generally preferred to sort through pain in solitude, could be consoled by a few pastel pieces of paper. *If you need anyone . . . I'm here for you . . . I want to be your friend.*

But a few years ago, when both my parents passed on within a year of each other and I had entered that strange, alternate universe which is grief, the cards began to come. On my desk at work. In my mailbox at home. Then a bouquet of flowers. A potted vine growing in the shape of a heart. A book of poetry. And with each gesture, I felt a layering of affection around me, felt tethered, safely, to the earth and those who loved me. Under each inadequate sentence I read: *There are no words of comfort. But I am here. I am here. I surround you with love.* I set the cards on bookshelves and tabletops and bedside tables, a sort of shield—made disarmingly and ordinarily of paper and painted flowers and gilded letters—against the forces that might push me toward the edge of insanity.

Just a few months after Patty's mother's murder, my family, too, was touched by violence. A stranger broke into our house and raped my mother. Thankfully, our crime did not make the newspapers, and, unlike Patty, I had the privilege of processing privately.

Almost privately. My mother contacted my and my sister's schools to tell our teachers what had happened, hoping they would understand our distraction, maybe ease up on the homework load, treat us with a conscious kindness. That, in itself, was unusual. My mother, ex-hippie and former teen rebel, tended to distrust schools, and whenever my sister or I complained about a teacher, she aligned with us and marched in to give that teacher a "piece of her mind." But mostly, as a busy, tired, single mother, she paid little attention to our schooling, with the exception of the occasional concert or required parent-teacher conference. Yet, here, in the middle of her own genuine devastation, my mother thought of us. She enlisted the community—weak as it was—to support us.

In those first few days back at school, when shock had erased my thoughts and I moved through the routines by rote alone, I don't remember how my teachers responded. I believe, thankfully, that they did not treat me differently nor pull me aside to ask how I was doing. I liked my teachers, trusted them, but our relationship was respectful, formal . . . they seemed to live on some far shore my boat would never reach, and I was too shy to be singled out for an awkward conversation. But I trusted that they held me in compassion; as I did math problems and took a history quiz, I felt them buoying me with their thoughts.

A few weeks later, my mother realized that she was too frightened to stay in our house and decided to move to my grandmother's in the neighboring town. On my last day in the school my English teacher—and here I share her real name, Mrs. Golder, Mrs. Janice Golder—decided to give me a going-away party.

Looking at her yearbook picture, I still can't guess Mrs. Golder's age. She is one of those teachers who seems to have always been a teacher. Her short brown hair is set in curls, like a grandmother's, but her skin is smooth and her face is strong and cheerful. She has a double chin, but I don't think of her as fat; instead, she is big. Big enough to fill up our room and keep us safe. She knows what she's doing. She never raises her voice and students never act out. We work hard for her.

In retrospect, it can't have been easy to be cheerful in our school, fraught as it was with its own dangers. The gangs that would later terrorize the high school had begun to shape and bully and bluster down the hallways. Doors automatically locked during passing periods to keep the teachers alone and safe in their rooms. Boys passed marijuana joints back and forth as they strutted down the corridors.

I didn't feel particularly close to anyone in my English class. We had all come from different elementary schools, students bussed from all over the city. I was at a particularly unattractive stage, with braces and pimples and a bad perm and no charisma to compensate. But I loved English. I wrote in my journal and waited for Mrs. Golder's comments. I eagerly learned grammar and devoted myself to her creative writing assignments. But I didn't notice my classmates

In Praise of Inadequate Gifts

and they didn't notice me. So the fact that Mrs. Golder had decided to give me a going away party was a bit of an embarrassment.

She brought a round, white cake with electric blue frosting trim and flowers. We milled about, eating. Without the structure of classroom routine, standing alone with my paper plate and plastic fork was pure awkwardness. Usually I loved food, especially piles of frosting, but because I was still in the after-tremors of shock, I couldn't taste anything. Also I felt a bit like Patty with her condolence card: I didn't believe anyone in the class had registered my existence before that moment. As soon as I left, my empty spot—like a hole in the sand when the tide comes in—would fill and the students would not remember me. Unlike Patty, this didn't pain me, but it made the party feel wrong. An inadequate gift.

Only it wasn't. Even then, through the fog of stunned grief, I was also profoundly, heartbreakingly touched. Not by the party, but by the gesture. Mrs. Golder couldn't say just the right words or take away what had happened, but she gave what she had. She used her precious personal time and money to buy a cake and donated her class period to honor me—and not even *me*, really, as I doubt I was more special to her than any other student. She did it because even an awkward eighth grade girl with braces and pimples and a bad perm deserves compassion.

The inclusive nature of her love touched me even more than if I'd been her favorite. The violence that had touched Patty and me was impersonal—and Mrs. Golder was the force of impersonal love fighting back against the broken people who had harmed us. In her action was a solidity, a grace, much larger than my awkward stance with my paper plate or the ugly blue stain of Crisco frosting on my lips. When I think back to eighth grade, the rape of my mother, the details of that night are tattooed forever in memory. But so is Mrs. Golder's party, an unlikely counterweight. Love's gestures are so unassuming, so ordinary, so clumsy, so imperfect—yet, miraculously, they hold something larger than themselves, big enough to press back against darkness.

Now that I, too, am an English teacher, I guess how difficult it must have been for Mrs. Golder, my mother's rape following so quickly on the heels of Patty's mother's murder. The suffering of our students rattles teachers, makes us feel inadequate. And I suspect this, too: that Mrs. Golder, in her many years of teaching hundreds and hundreds of students, probably does not remember that cake. Or me. And there is something beautiful in that, the love that gives without even the memory of it, like breath. Love that touches down, moves through a particular person at a particular time, then lifts. Love that might follow me anywhere, a constant shadowing companion.

Since my parents' deaths, I send condolence cards. Inadequate ones with cliché phrases. Like Patty's card, they may frustrate or offend, but perhaps they hold a little of Mrs. Golder's light. It's worth the risk.

The other day, I sat with a student after school to conference about her paper—a memoir about her depression and suicide attempt. Unlike my junior high, my affluent high school is rarely touched by crime, gang warfare, or even the scrappy after-school fights. Instead of threatening each other, our students harm themselves. They cut secret slices on their arms, starve themselves, dream of their own deaths. As teachers, we want to hold them, to save them, but they cannot see us. Our gifts are weak and insufficient.

So I asked my student, who is just stretching her way toward healing, "What helped?" She remembered all her friends who encouraged her, who argued for life, even when she was too sullen and withdrawn to respond. Although they were not in the room, she spoke directly to them: "When you were talking, you thought I couldn't hear you, but I heard you. I heard you."

Then she was quiet, and turned to me. "Just being there. Physically. Being there. You don't have to say anything at all."

ACKNOWLEDGMENTS

I am proud and pleased to be associated with Wandering Aengus Press. Founder Jill McCabe Johnson is an inspiration; I am in awe of her sense of possibility, her contributions to the arts community, and her stunning combination of gentleness and fierce courage. Julie Riddle was a dream editor: brilliant, intuitive, skilled, and compassionate. The book is much improved for her insight.

I am so moved by artist Laura Deem's willingness to share her perfect image for the cover. Please visit her website to explore more of her work: https://www.lauradeemstudio.com

Praise be to the generous teams at literary magazines. Denton Loving and Darnell Arnoult edited "My Perfect Little Life" for *Drafthorse*; Jan Becker edited "Loveland" for *Gulf Stream*; Ken Weisner and his students edited "Disaster Man" for *Red Wheelbarrow*; Amy Lowe edited "A Narrative Break" for *Ruminate*; Amy Butcher edited "In Praise of Old Laundromats" for *Defunct*; Luc Saunders edited "Faithful Over a Few Things" for *The Sun*; the talented team at River Teeth edited *Why We Don't Have Children*, and Wendy McDowell edited "In Praise of Inadequate Gifts" for *Harvard Divinity Bulletin*.

Jenny Munro, one of my favorite people in the universe, generously lent her eagle eye and keen grammar skills to the final edits.

During the years I crafted these essays, I was supported by my faithful, astute, and big-hearted writing group: Jan Stites, Mike Karpa, Madelon Phillips, Wendy Schultz, and Melinda Maxwell-Smith. How grateful I am that Jan Stites—lo those many years ago—wrapped me into her fold, took me seriously as a writer, and gave me a practical and inspiring model for how to finish a book.

Pamela Kaye read some early drafts, buoyed me through my fears and doubts, and shared her writing retreat in Cambria, where Randi Browning joined us. I first met my professor Randi when I was eighteen and she has shaped, more than anyone, how I think about teaching and writing.

I am profoundly grateful for the vision of Stan Rubin and Judith Kitchen, founders of the Rainier Writing Workshop. Judith was a life-transforming mentor, whose work continues to stun me and whose belief in me continues to carry me. Judith hand-matched me with two other gifted mentors who taught me, not only craft, but how to live a writers' life with courage, integrity, and generosity: Brenda Miller and Peggy Shumaker.

May every writer have a Lita Kurth in their lives. Her well-timed, wise words give me belief in the value of this work. She has a rare talent: the ability to provide meaningful guidance on every stage of the writing process. She continually inspires me with the range and originality in her writing, her generosity in her teaching, and the faithfulness with which she lives her values. Our weekly writing dates have been a sustaining touchstone.

A shout-out to my accountability partners: For over a decade, Sarah Tiederman and I have shared weekly life-goals and reflections. For the last three years, Tania Martin and I shared weekly writing goals and encouragement by email, which has kept me honest and helped me feel companioned. For the last six weeks of final edits on this manuscript, Justin Chu and I met by Zoom every morning to write together and motivate each other.

Lucky me, for mysterious reasons the late Michael Steinberg, great advocate of creative nonfiction, decided to adopt me as a mentee and had an angel-like gift of discerning what I needed most to hear.

Ginny Moyer, fellow writer and teacher, has been unflagging in her support and in her wise insights into various drafts. Knowing that my dear friend, the poet Kasey Jueds, is on this journey with me, is a constant source of courage. Hilary Schafer inspires me with her gentle wisdom. Marc Vincenti continues to be a teacher for me—and has the uncanny knack of sending me just the right words at the moment I most need them. I continue to be energized and inspired by conversations about craft and the writing life with Jim Hessler.

These friends did not give feedback on these essays, but their belief in me carried me through difficult stages of the writing—and my life—and was more important than they will ever realize: June Riley, Angela Dellaporta, Karen Meyers, Diane Ichickawa, Lynne Navarro, Deanna Messinger, Kristy Blackburn, Paul Dunlap, Ellen Feigenbaum, Roni Habib, Allison Shotwell, Kasey O'Connell, and Andrea Robicheau. Martha Elderon read and celebrated every essay and always asked for more.

Thank you to my sister, Rima, who has allowed me to tell her

In Praise of Inadequate Gifts

story along with mine, and who lives her life with whole-heartedness and resilience.

Then there are those people—especially important to those of us whose biological families are small and fragmented—who adopt us and are a steady ground from which we can heal and do hard work. I thank my forever friends Debbie Gotchef and Tom Haak. Lynda Matthias, also chosen family, has been my unofficial one-woman marketing firm and continues to inspire me with her commitment to community and the arts and her talent for making strangers into friends. The Kato family continues to be a heart-center.

I married that younger man from the essays, Christopher Bell, and am more grateful than words can say for his care and support and for our many quiet joys. He makes adventures more magical and ordinary days feel like gifts.

CPSIA information can be obtained
at www.ICGtesting.com
Printed in the USA
FSHW021047250621
82703FS

9 780578 868950